Chasing After the Wind:

A Journey of Faith

by

Susan "Micki" Digby

Dedication:

For my daughters, Denise and Jenifer
What we share sets us apart

Acknowledgements

Thank you to Jenifer Jill Digby Gile . . . but there are no words that adequately convey the feelings I have of gratitude. There would be no words written if Jill did not see them first. All I did was tell my story to one who was willing to listen and craft it into sentences that made sense. This book belongs to Jill as much as it does to me. Thank you for your patience and clarity, your encouragement every step of the way. This must be what it feels like to have a sister, one who just won't let you go.

Many thanks also to Alison Gile, my nephew's wife, who offered her design expertise to the format and printing of this narrative. The transformation of word to book – this polished and beautiful volume – could not have taken place without her.

Table of Contents

Foreword to Micki's Story

by

Jenifer Jill Digby Gile

As I approached my 60th birthday, it occurred to me that I should set down some of my memories, so that my children and grandchildren would have a record of the events that formed me, and, to some extent, them. I was inspired by the memories my mother shared, toward the end of her life, but also by another form of reflection that had recently inspired millions: "The Last Lecture" as delivered by CMU professor, Randy Pausch. For an ongoing series at Carnegie Mellon University, top academics at the height of their careers were asked to think deeply about what mattered to them, and then give a hypothetical "final talk" with a topic such as "what wisdom would you try to impart to the world if you knew it was your last chance?" Although he was only 46 in September, 2007, Pausch's talk, "Really Achieving Your Childhood Dreams" was not hypothetically final – he'd recently been diagnosed with an aggressive form of cancer – pancreatic – and had been given only a short time to live. The lecture video went viral, an abbreviated version appeared on *Oprah*, and the talk in book form was published in April, 2008, all before Pausch finally succumbed to his disease in October 2009, leaving a widow and three young children. "The Last Lecture" of Randy Pausch was brilliant, funny, wry, moving, and ultimately life-affirming. In the case of his youngest child, born after his diagnosis, it will be the only voice of her father she'll ever hear.

Just after I finished the first version of my own "last lecture," *Finding My Voice*, a close friend of ours was diagnosed with terminal cancer. He, too, was given mere months to live, but David had a young, second family and a will to fight, and the story of his survival, and his recent designation: *cured* – a word almost never assigned to a Stage IV cancer patient – is nothing short of miraculous. In the beginning, though, he believed the prognosis he'd been given, and he had some things to say, he just wasn't sure how to say them. I mentioned "The Last Lecture" to his wife Carla, along with another form of memoir I'd recently heard about, the "ethical will." The term is somewhat puzzling, because it doesn't describe a legal document like a Last Will and Testament, and I'm not quite sure how ethics come into it, but if you suspect at times that lawyers and ethics have little in common, maybe the designation "ethical will" begins to make sense as an alternate, philosophical document – not a disposition of goods, but a disposition of ideas. In essence, it's still a memoir, a collection of the thoughts you'd like to pass on to your family after you're gone.

As it happened, David and Carla were planning to travel from Anchorage to Denver to visit two of his older children, and I suggested that he organize his thoughts and we'd then record them via VideoCam. I sent him a series of questions to think about, prompts to guide his memory and encompass the hopes and wishes he had for all who would survive him.

David was visibly nervous as we sat in our living room and turned on the recorder – we all were – and I anticipated having to draw out his thoughts by repeating the prompts and feeding him follow-up questions to keep the flow going. In the event, David got started and didn't stop talking for almost four hours. There were tears – his and ours – but at least as much laughter, and considerable awe. He delved into the past, confessed some deep regrets, spoke of the things he was most proud of. It was a remarkable, cathartic, experience.

At about the same time that David was beginning his epic cancer journey, my sister-in-law, Micki Digby, began hers. Diagnosed with lung cancer in December, 2009, she too was given a grim prognosis. Like David, she pursued every avenue of treatment open to her: surgery, radiation, chemotherapy, gene therapy, nutritional therapy, immunotherapy. Her trajectory, however, rarely deviated from downwards. Although she certainly outlived the original predictions, even had a few brief remissions, her cancer drove on relentlessly, eventually metastasizing to her adrenals and the bones of her spine. She entered hospice care in September, 2017, but then took a sabbatical of sorts to undergo radiation once again – not for any chance of a cure, but because radiation can be palliative for the incredible pain experienced once cancer enters the bones. When that failed, she re-entered hospice.

Several years earlier, I had spent some time with Micki while my husband Marshall and my two brothers, Michael and Richard (her husband), went to Mystic for a course in celestial navigation. Originally, we'd talked of all going to Connecticut, but Micki's disease had progressed to a point where energy was at a low ebb, so I decided to keep her company at their home near Philadelphia while the men went north to sail. It had been years since we'd spent much time together, but even under the circumstances of her failing health, it was a serene and companionable experience. I let her dictate the pace; she needed a long nap every afternoon, and went to bed, as a rule, right after the nightly news, but during the days we'd chat and prepare meals together, and even took a few short local excursions. I went with her to choir practice at her church – she was still trying to participate as often as possible – and sang beside her at the service that Sunday morning.

While I was with Micki, we talked about recording memories – about the ideas behind the "ethical will" and the "last lecture." She'd already read my own collection of family lore and legends, and it seemed to her that writing about her cancer journey might be well worth the effort, both as a legacy for her family, but also as therapy for herself. When I got home, I sent her a couple of books about writing an ethical will, and both she and Richard were excited about the idea. She promised to send me something – soon. I had almost given up, though, when the first packet of longhand pages arrived in the mail. She'd collected some scraps of thoughts and poetry, jotted a few notes to herself, and then began an actual narrative. I was to be her editor for the project.

For almost three years we worked on the memoir, and at times I thought I myself would despair and have to abandon the project. Almost everything she wrote seemed completely negative to me – discouraging, depressing. I myself went through cancer diagnosis and treatment during this time, admittedly with a much less threatening form of the disease, but I don't ever remember feeling like this:

> *You can't see my pain.*
> *I can't go on.*
> *I go on.*

Or this:

> *Life slips away from you while you're standing in a grocery line waiting to pay for a quart of milk. Time passes and takes everything in its path: youth, hopes, dreams. Dreams. It takes them most of all.*

———

> *Alone.*

You are alone. Alone in your head, thinking, worrying, wondering: Why me? How come now? What's going to happen? Am I going to die? All the questions you'll never stop asking and have no answer to.

No matter how many people you surround yourself with, cancer is a solitary event. This is the deep reality that you are sharing this experience only with yourself. This is one of the most painful realizations of your having cancer. It hits you in the most unusual places – in a room filled with noise and lots of activity. It's nothing monumental or earth-shattering, but you are saddened to your core. No matter how hard you, and those around you, try, you are ultimately in this alone. They could never know or feel exactly the emotions that churn through you. I often feel this aloneness is a driving force to our survival. In loneliness, there is strength.

When this aloneness first hits, it is strange and frightening. But this sense of isolation will become a part of my new life. It is up to me; I am in this alone; I have to work harder than ever! I am fighting for my own survival.

I resisted transcribing these ideas, partly to save the feelings of my brother, who approached Micki's illness with Churchillian resolve: "Never, never, never, never, never give up!" It seemed to me Richard deserved more credit for his positive outlook and the unwavering support he gave his wife. I cut out one paragraph that I thought might be particularly hurtful, but in time I came to realize that this was Micki's memoir, not mine, and this was how she perceived pain and faced death. A remarkable clear-sightedness, in fact, informed much of what she wrote. I needed – she needed – her voice to be heard, not mine.

Occasionally, I was able to persuade Micki to add an amusing story, something about her past life that hadn't been subsumed in her present suffering. I asked for, and eventually got, a passage about my brother Richard, whose sunny, optimistic disposition had been her bulwark through the darkest hours. She wrote about how opposite they were in the way they saw the world, and I realized that this difference was probably the secret to their enduring marriage – 50 years in December, 2017. They complemented each other.

I regret that I was never able to get her to write about a mystery in her genetic heritage. Family tradition held that her maternal grandparents, and therefore her mother, were full Cherokee, which would have explained the beautiful structure of Micki's face, and also, perhaps, her strength of mind and her somewhat stoic temperament. However, she'd long resisted exploring the connection, and, when given a DNA kit, declined to use it. Perhaps she worried that her Native American origins had been exaggerated, or even invented. On the other hand, it could have been that the scars of prejudice ran too deep. She remembered, from earliest childhood, her mother admonishing her always to be clean and tidy, so that she would never be called a "dirty Indian." Had her mother been called that? It seems likely. To me, she would say only that she had no desire to revisit that part of her past.

Even when I persuaded her to tell a happy story, she'd often end it with a reality check: what she used to do that she could no longer do; things she'd enjoyed, now denied to her; places she'd never go again; anxiety that plagued and paralyzed her. Interspersed in the narrative were quotes from scripture and poems that inspired her. The title itself, *Chasing After the Wind*, was taken from a passage in Ecclesiastes. Still resisting her feelings of isolation, I suggested the inclusion of "You'll Never Walk Alone" and she immediately agreed to put it in. Without saying more, we both considered that one day I might sing it at her memorial service. In spite of what I saw as negativity and she probably felt was a firm grip on reality, a rock-solid Christian faith continued to give her consolation, and hope. The first version of the memoir, which I thought was probably complete in April, 2018, ended with this:

> *It is my hope that my family will finally find peace and learn to carry on in productive ways. I feel the need to apologize for the eight-year nightmare I've put them through. They need to know I wish them happiness in their lives – not perfection – just simple, "aha" moments to live by. I also want them to know that if I can, I will ask God to guide their steps.*

My daughter-in-law, Alison, a graphic designer, worked with me to format and self-publish the original. At my husband's urging, I flew to Philadelphia that spring, taking six copies, handsomely bound in a cover of sky blue and heavenly clouds. Marshall was convinced that Micki should hold the book in her hands before she died. My surprise visit was a gamble, as she was really struggling with visitors, but it proved a joy to both of us.

Although I felt the memoir was complete, Micki continued to live, and continued to write, so we began to talk cautiously about a second edition, with perhaps a wider distribution. She wanted her journey to be in some way helpful to others. It was also more and more obvious that one of the things that was keeping her alive, past all expectations, hospice extensions, and a relentless spiral of pain, was writing.

I continue to believe that Micki's cancer journey, despite what she has written, was never really taken alone. My brother travelled with her; Denise and Jenifer, her wonderful daughters; their husbands and their children, were beside her much of the way. For the past few years, I've been there too, trying to understand, and to learn. I think she has given me a precious gift: I now can see the tremendous courage it took for Micki to face her fears, and her inevitable death, and write from her heart. I'm not sure I could ever equal her bravery, or attain her clear vision, but I admired her, and I am eternally grateful that she allowed me into her mind, and her heart. I will never forget her example. I know she has found peace.

I've now written, read, prompted, edited, or participated in a number of memoirs. I started my own, not with any hope of a larger audience – who outside my immediate family could possibly care about some of this minutiae, I wondered – but I did think that the origins of our personal myths and legends were worth setting down for my family, my children, and theirs. Beyond that, the exercise proved deeply satisfying in other ways. I was able to revisit some happy times, and lay to rest some ghosts. Ultimately, by recording those musings, I hoped my children would hear my voice someday, as I can still hear my mother's in the wonderful memories she sketched for us, so characteristic of her good sense, and her great sense of humor. I hope Micki's words, perhaps more of a journal than a memoir, will yet prove an example and an inspiration to others, whether they are facing a terminal disease or simply trying to gather and record their memories and thoughts.

The creation of a personal narrative – call it what you will – can help you manage the present or bring the past alive, in a way that can be gratifying to oneself, but more importantly, to those we leave behind.

As I said to Micki all those years ago: It's your story – why not pass it on? Find your voice, and let it sing. I believe she did.

At Liberty
Denver, Colorado
October 2018

Chasing After the Wind:

A Journey of Faith

by

Susan "Micki" Digby

As a title to these reflections, I'd like to borrow a phrase used repeatedly in Ecclesiastes. "Chasing After the Wind" describes my cancer journey every step of the way, with one exception: Providence. Or maybe two: Providence and Faith. In thinking about what I've experienced, I'm reminded also of this Bible verse: "When I was a child I thought as a child . . . " The naiveté of the newly-diagnosed; you have no idea what you don't know. This is a whole new world to you. And you begin chasing the wind the moment you sign your first release form.

Ecclesiastes says all of life is meaningless. I do not subscribe to this idea. However, I do see now that what I thought was important, like my work, was something that could be done by others. I wasn't irreplaceable. Many people pour themselves into their work and neglect those closest to them. In the end – who is there for you if not your family? In a part of your life, you amass things, only to find them meaningless later. Work evaporates. Things become mundane and unimportant. Chasing work – chasing things – was chasing after the wind.

The first two months of this ordeal – or call it a journey – were a nightmare. I had surgery to remove the upper lobe of my right lung. My mindset was: "Well, I'll do the surgery and recover and get back to my life." I was so certain of this I never gave it another thought. But I was chasing the wind – and I would never catch it. Then came chemo and radiation and I did this with the same mindset: "I'll get through this and then get back to my life." There I was again, chasing after the wind. Another year later, when the cancer returned, we did genetic testing and found that I have the KRAS mutation. I also found out what that means: no matter what they do with treatment, the cancer will always come back. And so I saw in my mind's eye, I would spend the rest of my life, "chasing after the wind." This is what hope is all about – chasing something that you believe you can achieve. I lost hope many times, sometimes for weeks at a time, and then I would go on again – not always sure, but I guess I was hoping against hope that I could catch that wind.

———

You can't see my pain.
I can't go on.
I go on.

———

I never believed I was given this disease so that I would do something good with it. We make our own choices in spite of what life hits us with. Be positive, we're told.
I wasn't always positive – my choice.

———

I really do not want to write all of this. Why? Because I am one lone voice out there among all the hurting souls in this world. Who cares what my challenges have been and still are? However – and this is a big however – not one day goes by that I don't think of these things and I am drawn, so strongly, to paper and pen. (Is that you, Jill? Did God send me Jill to nag and encourage and cajole these reflections out of me?) Does God want me to record my thoughts so that maybe they will help someone else? I don't really understand the strong and persistent nudging to write. But I must. I am being called.

Over time, I have jotted thoughts down, here, there, and everywhere. I read incessantly also, and finding a word or phrase that speaks to me – I just jot these things down also. They are all mixed into my notes, and I certainly don't want to be accused of plagiarism. But a private journal is just that – personal to me and a few of my loved ones – so I'm sure the blend of my thoughts with others' cannot be considered anything beyond a very personal mix of musings and memories, thoughts and inspirations.

———

2017: Looking Back on My Journey

In October of 2009 I began this trip – not knowing why or where it would lead me because, up to that year, surgery of any nature, to my mind, was not an option. For some reason, I began to look into surgery, for my feet and for hemorrhoids. Why? These were both inconveniences that I had lived with for years. And this had been my mindset for 30-plus years – since my bout with cancer at age 29 – at which time I vowed: No More Surgery Ever! So why begin this? I'm still not certain, but I do believe I was being led down this path.

As I pursued each of these various surgeries, collecting information, I began to notice a pattern with my blood pressure. It was always a wee bit high – surprising to me, especially since I have always had low blood pressure. I was always shocked by each episode of elevated BP, and so each nurse who confronted me with the numbers would always brush it off as "white coat syndrome," better-known as fear. After this recurred several times, I thought it best to see my primary physician and just check into it. He sent me to have a heart CAM done at the University of Pennsylvania on October 31, 2009.

A week or so following this procedure, I had not received my results, so I called to ask their whereabouts. I was told some story about the doctor who read them failing to sign them before leaving on vacation. Another week passed and I called again. They seemed flustered, but said they would mail the results to my doctor. Another week went by. I called my doctor and the Heart Center, asking for my results: "not available." At last, on the evening before Thanksgiving, at 9:30 PM, my doctor called to say he received a FAX of my results and all was "wonderful" with my heart. The following Saturday, in the mail, I received the written copy of the results and at the very bottom of the copy, as a footnote, actually, I read that a CT Scan was suggested because of a "possible lung mass."

As is usually the case, I had to wait until Monday to reconnect with my primary care physician. Past experience with cancer and its treatments surely taught me the need for patience. When I contacted my primary doctor on Monday, I was fit to be tied – why hadn't he told me about this possible lung mass? As it turned out, this footnote did not appear on his copy. It turns out that when I signed all those consent forms I also signed something that said they couldn't tell me anything outside the heart results. So apparently at least one person had struggled with having this information and not being able to share it with me. To this person, I say: Thank You! You gave me many more years to enjoy life.

———

Life slips away from you while you're standing in a grocery line waiting to pay for a quart of milk. Time passes and takes everything in its path: youth, hopes, dreams. Dreams. It takes them most of all.

———

Alone.
You are alone. Alone in your head, thinking, worrying, wondering: Why me? How come now? What's going to happen? Am I going to die? All the questions you'll never stop asking and have no answer to.

No matter how many people you surround yourself with,

cancer is a solitary event. This is the deep reality that you are sharing this experience only with yourself. This is one of the most painful realizations of your having cancer. It hits you in the most unusual places – in a room filled with noise and lots of activity. It's nothing monumental or earth-shattering, but you are saddened to your core. No matter how hard you, and those around you, try, you are ultimately in this alone. They could never know or feel exactly the emotions that churn through you. I often feel this aloneness is a driving force to our survival. In loneliness, there is strength. When this aloneness first hits, it is strange and frightening. But this sense of isolation will become a part of my new life. It is up to me; I am in this alone; I have to work harder than ever! I am fighting for my own survival.

My first two surgeries removed the lymph nodes in the middle of my chest and the top lobe of my lung. I'd been in the hospital only four days, but since there was an impending snowstorm, and I was deemed to be doing so well, I was released and sent home. What a comedy of errors followed that decision! Within hours of arriving home, we lost power. It was February, and it was cold! Rich was lighting fires for heat and candles for light all over the house. Adding to the "atmosphere" was the large array of flowers I had received, all of which made it hard for me to breathe. Late on the second night, Jenifer showed up to rescue us and take us home with her. We stayed two days – and all the while I was getting weaker. We came home once the power was back on, but I was having more and more trouble breathing. In short order, I ended up back in the hospital with a collapsed lung and internal bleeding.

A third surgery was required – going back in through the original incision to inflate the lung and stop the bleeding. One day after this surgery, I began leaking lymphatic fluid. Anything I ate or drank was not being processed, but was "third spacing" throughout my body. I began to look like the "Poppin' Fresh dough girl." All food and drink was stopped and I was fed intravenously. This went on for four weeks while I had more surgeries to fix the leaks. The top thoracic surgeon must have discovered that my middle name was Louise, because he started calling me "Louie the Leak," as I walked the halls, trailing my pole and all its attached paraphernalia.

These surgeries involved going in through the feet, threading cameras up into the chest cavity. Once a leak was found, it was sealed off with glue and platinum. (It's quite a necklace I have now in my chest – showing up clearly on x-rays.) I was so thirsty. I wanted to drink anything I could get, but I wasn't even allowed ice. Eventually I enlisted an unsuspecting nurse to be my accomplice. I convinced her it would be okay to give me a small glass of water along with a packet of Metamucil to help me eliminate. (Little did we realize there was nothing to eliminate. Duh.) I drank that water down as fast as I could swallow! Later that day, I was scheduled for another procedure to find and patch the leaks. This was so funny: The cameras are in place and the doctor and I are looking at the monitor. Lo and behold! There's the telltale evidence, floating around. The doctor says to me, "What's that?" and right before I went out, I replied, "Metamucil." Oh, my. The look on his face – priceless!

———

God says, "If you suffer, I'll give you the grace to go forward."

What God asks of men is faith. His invisibility is the truest test of faith. To know who sees him, God makes himself unseen.

Why can't we remember God's grace?

When I was 29 and diagnosed with cervical cancer, Dr. Densmore sat me down and told me some things that were very strange to me at that time. But first, let me say that I received that call on July 23rd, my 29th birthday.

"You have cancer and we need to work together on this."

That's all I knew. When we talked, she told me she needed me to be on her side – not to be denying this. Not to be feeling sorry for myself. To do this, she would work me through the grief process – grief for my own dying. Only then could I get to the point of acceptance – and then I could live. After that process, I truly turned the corner and was willing to take the next step.

The next step was to visualize all the cells lining up just the way God made them – healthy and strong. Not seeing (in my mind's eye) any cancer. She taught me how to see this – showing me pictures so I could see too. After 2 months, she did the surgery, a hysterectomy, and at last! No cancer.

So when I got the lung cancer diagnosis, why did I forget God's grace? Was I too sick, too tired, too ready to give up? I went through therapy after therapy, chemo and radiation, surgery, more chemo, more radiation. I was so beat down, sometimes I did give up and thought dying would be easier. I actually accepted dying as the only way. When I was diagnosed with PTSD in 2015, I met Donna, my therapist. She gave me a script to read and after a couple of visits, asked what I thought of the script. It was a script of visualization and healing. I was once again reminded of God's grace. Donna said if I would like to do this, she would help me. I said a resounding "Yes!" I believe in this. I told her the story of when I did this at age 29, and the results. So God sent me another person to help me heal. Wow! I am blessed. Donna asked if I wanted to use "the universe" or "God" or a "higher being" in the script. I said "God!" She said, "Good, I am a Christian, too. Let's get started."

I had tried on my own and felt less than able to draw upon the healing, but when she agreed to help me in my weakness, I felt the healing begin. We did this only twice, but when my doctor asked me if I wanted to see my new PET scan – he was almost jumping up and down – so excited – the cancer in my left lung and lower lobe of my right lung were gone! The tumor was shrinking. This was after 4 months of immunotherapy. I didn't want to burst his bubble and tell him: God had a big role in this. It wasn't all your doing.

Looking back at Dr. Densmore, I see now that she was quite a unique person – a form of Providence in my life even then. She told me once that she put herself through medical school at the University of Pennsylvania by driving the trolley at night. She did a comparative study on the nutritional content of cat food vs. dog food, and so, with little money, she dined on the latter. When I was 19 I had evidence of possible reproductive problems, so she suggested that if I wanted children at all, I'd better think of getting started. Richard and I figured we could get married and two could live cheaper than one. Ah, youth! Dr. Densmore went on to deliver both of our daughters, and because we had no insurance, she charged us a mere $70 to deliver our first. Of course, our second child came with insurance and a job. And sure enough, six years later, I had my first experience with cancer. By the way, Dr. Densmore left medicine and moved to Maine, where she teaches people to fly.

———

I have had so many of my hopes dashed away. Do I continue to hope for some miracle or do I get myself ready for . . . the inevitable?

I am always wanting to clean out drawers, clothes, all that I see. I want to give things away. I am obsessed with getting rid of things. To simplify. To make it easier for those left behind?

Coming face to face with death, everything changed. Nothing changed.

Waiting to live. Deferred gratification.

Waiting to die. Patience.

———

August 10, 2010

Hope is the thing with feathers
That perches in the soul,
And sings the tune without the words,
And never stops at all
— Emily Dickinson

How beautiful I felt those words were. I had to keep them for posterity. It's what I feel – most of the time.

———

2011: Survivors

I did not want to join a support group for cancer patients –

survivors – as we are called. But emotionally, I knew that I wasn't healthy, so I looked up one close to me and attended. Well. I was in a state of shock, because when I began to tell my story, everything came tumbling out. I talked for 2 hours and the best thing was, they listened, attentively, and asked me questions that were right on. I found a home there and six years later I still go twice a month. The one thing that struck me and has stayed with me till today – I was searching so strongly to get my life back. I wanted more than anything to have my life back. One of the other folks attending the group told me straight out: this was my new normal. After you have been diagnosed with cancer, there is no turning back. You are either dealing with it daily or anticipating the next scan. Little did I know at that time. I'd had 5 surgeries only in that first year – no chemo – no radiation. I thought I would gradually get stronger and back to being me.

———

2011-2012

After the first year, my cancer reappeared and I found out from genetic testing that I had the KRAS mutation. KRAS has been studied and researched for over 20 years, but in that time there have yet to be any good results that I am aware of. KRAS mutation means that they can treat the cancer until there is no evidence of disease, yet, in my case, every year it has come back. The recurrence was a low point for me. That year I did chemo and radiation every three weeks and radiation for 40 days. More than three months of treatment followed by three months of recovery from treatment – 6 months out of each year – that was what I had to look forward to. I was one sick puppy! And another piece of my life was disappearing. Of course, I didn't recognize it at the time. Only later did I realize how weak I was. No muscle tone; I was unable to do the simplest things; afraid of having to defend myself. So I went to physical therapy and it helped to get stronger and I began regular exercise after that. Until the next time – the third time, I heard: Your cancer is back.

2012

This time, it wasn't so bad – a spot on the lower lobe – no biopsy, just radiation – SBRT or Stereotactic Body Radiation Therapy – only 5 times, and I was good to go. Just fatigue.

I am always running out of energy. I just hit a wall. There is no reserve. I don't get a second wind. I either go to sleep or limp through the rest of the day. Getting my bath after dinner bothers me. I used to almost start a new day after dinner, working until 12 or 1 o'clock. Now, bed time is 10:30 and I do little in the evening. People try to push me, thinking because I look the same on the outside, I must be the same on the inside. I wonder some days how in the world did I end up here? The fatigue is extreme but it is my new normal. I do accept the fatigue; it seems to have won over depressions.

I used to watch my mother-in-law sit on the couch and stare at the floor. I always wondered about that. Now I know, because I do the same. I am either finding rest or not wanting to respond to something recently said. I suspect it was the same with her.

———

Cancer changes all your relationships.

I needed some help – with all I was doing, couldn't other folks figure out their role?

I've lost my identity as a person. Who am I now? To relate to others seemed vague. Men often experience this after leaving a job that somehow defined them.

———

No, I am not fine.

———

One thing that really bothers me: God didn't give me cancer. I don't blame God. (So how could I wonder why he won't heal me?) There are too many contributing factors:

1. My Dad had lung cancer. It was before they did genetic testing, so how do I know if he also had the KRAS mutation that I also have? Was it hereditary?

2. We have lived for over 40 years in a home with very high levels of radon. Never thought about getting it tested until after I was diagnosed.

3. I smoked, but so did Richard and everyone I knew then.

So how could I blame God? But I do wonder If he could heal me, and if so, why doesn't he? Does he heal some people and not others for a bigger purpose?

———

2013-2014

Another year went by, very quiet, and then my fourth diagnosis. This time, back to chemotherapy and proton therapy (40 days again). Sick all over again. Very sick. Six more months and then atrophy to overcome. Back to the gym to rebuild my physical body. Mentally, I never really gave up, but I wanted to many times! If I had to tell you why I haven't given up, the only reason I can think of is my faith. You see, back in 2010, when I had all those surgeries in less than one month, I was physically and mentally beat up. I had hit bottom. I was actually willing to die. I was scheduled for my 6th surgery, and that evening I prayed. I told God I was done, I couldn't go on – no more surgeries – and so I gave it up to Him. I fell into a deep and relaxed sleep. I don't think I ever had such a peaceful night's sleep since entering the hospital. In the morning, I woke to my surgeon standing by my bed and he said to me, "I have cancelled your surgery for today. Looks like you have healed yourself." And I replied, "Thank you, but I already know that." Did I know before he talked with me? No, but when I opened my eyes and looked at him, I knew.

I've had two occasions like this in my life. This was the more recent. In my teenage years, I was confirmed at church. We were members of the Episcopalian faith, and so the Bishop came in to confirm the young people of the church. I can remember to this day, when the Bishop laid his hands on me, I felt this warm feeling throughout my body and I was so moved, I began to cry. When I looked around, no one else was crying, and they all were looking at me. I regained my composure and nothing was ever said, but I have never forgotten that feeling and that day,

———

2015-2016

One year after this horrendous treatment my cancer was still quiet. My oncologist wanted to put me on a maintenance chemo "for the rest of my life." I just wasn't ready for more chemo, especially "for the rest of my life. " What if I lost my hair again? What if I was sick again? For the rest of my life?

About this same time, one of my daughters introduced me to a woman whose life work was to help people like me through a nutritional program. She encouraged me to show it to my doctor, to get her blessing, and to follow me with scans and blood work. My oncologist turned me down. I wanted to try something besides chemo, so I found another oncologist who looked at the protocol and told me a lot of the elements were in clinical trial, so yes, he would help me. This protocol gave me six months of good scans and freedom from treatments, but, as always, the cancer came back – a fifth time.

After this recurrence, I began immunotherapy. For the first four months, we saw no change, and it was thought that it wasn't working for me. Then, at one doctor's appointment, he noticed my hands and said, "Oh, good! You have RA." Rheumatoid Arthritis. Not so good, if you ask me. But it meant that the immune therapy had revved up my immune system, and now I was developing autoimmune diseases.

But the cancer was receding; it appeared to have disappeared from my left lung and the major tumor in my right

24

middle lobe was smaller. I stayed on this course until June of 2016, when I heard, "This treatment is no longer working, so we are stopping it." The autoimmune diseases, RA and dermatitis, however, were now front and center. So I began this next 9 months with scans every 2 months and slow-growing cancer that played tricks with my mind the entire time. I never really enjoyed this "time off." Now that I am losing weight rapidly and the cancer is back in the left lung, I am in constant pain. I take so many pills, it scares me. Can you believe I take morphine and another opioid? Me? Up to eight years ago, I never even took aspirin. Is this the new me? The time is coming for me to say yes or no. How will I know how to answer?

———

January 2017: Hallelujah

Just last week, my sister-in-law from Alaska was in town, and she came for a short visit. Unbeknownst to me, she was also delivering a Christmas gift from her daughter, my niece Sarah. The gift was a video that they had produced, telling the story of my journey with cancer. It turns out that one year ago, while we were in Alaska, I told Sarah of my love for the music of Leonard Cohen's "Hallelujah," and I said I would love to see her skate to that music.

Sarah is now living in LA and working with several elite coaches. She is a beautiful skater. So a video arrived, and we were so touched. Yes, it is beautiful to watch, but the message it brought to me was that they, way up there in Alaska, cared about me. We cried and cried and continue to cry every time we watch the video. For once in a long time, I felt that I wasn't alone. When you have cancer, you are alone in so many ways, because no one can truly understand, no one can "see" your pain. I finally felt like someone gets it: Sarah and LuAnn, because, knowingly or not, they captured my feelings so well.

———

Courage is fear that has said its prayers.
— Karle Wilson Baker

———

Talking to Family

I attended a support group one day and the nurse facilitator was unable to come, so she sent a social worker in her place. This was the first and only time I began crying when it was my turn to talk. Well, one thing I have learned: don't show your emotions to a social worker because they will have you in therapy before you know what's happening. And I really didn't want another appointment with anyone. She said something though that caught my attention. She said maybe she could tell me something that would cause me to think differently about my situation. And she gave me her card. That card sat on my desk and haunted me. I kept looking at it every time I sat down and finally, about a month later, I picked up the phone and made an appointment to see her. As always, my husband attended (he has not missed one of my appointments).

What the social worker did was to see that we were not sharing with our family. I was doing what I believed was good; I was protecting them. Well, she pointed out to us that our kids and grandkids were reacting the same; they were protecting us from their pain and wondering. And so the elephant in the room was growing.

Almost the next day I began talking with each one and the relief I saw from my two daughters was immediate and tearful. I felt better and they surely did. Communication was open and flowing once again (after nearly six years of hiding our feelings from each other). Then, one by one, I had lunch with my two older grandkids – we met separately so they could talk to me, too. When I met with my two sons-in-law, they were grateful for my honesty and for caring how they felt. The best was my youngest grandson who was 9 at the time. I told him the same as I told the others: "I love you and want you to know that I am sick. Also, please know that I will always be truthful. I will tell you the truth and I want you to ask me anything you wonder about, at any time." So first he said, "Well, my mom told me not to ask you about your cancer," to which I assured him he could. In fact, did he have anything to ask me now? He replied, "Are you coming to watch my game on Saturday?" I'm not sure he understood, but I went to his game.

———

Liquid Stars

A Tanka Sequence

by Pamela A. Babusci

praying
all day & all night
to God
never questioning why
cancer invaded my life

until the doctor
tells me what stage cancer
i have, my fears
will hang like dewdrops
on a bleeding heart

pale gray clouds
across the morning star
i gather
strength & courage
for my first chemo

wishing my mother
was here to hold my hand
during treatments
from beyond life
i can feel her blessing

after chemo
getting thinner & thinner
my body
its shadow
fading on the wall

hair falling out
in clumps in my brush
on the floor
like petals
of a dying lotus

cancer is merely
a detour in life…
walking down
a nameless road
i stop & pick wild violets

no way off
this cancer journey
i set sail
into the blue batik sky
& glide without wings

autumn leaves
shedding into the misty day
slowly, slowly
my hair
growing back

who will rebuild
the ruins of my heart
after cancer?
i scoop up liquid stars
& drink them

Richard

I have to say I am blessed in so many ways, having the family I have, but my husband outdoes them all. You know, I've found that about 75% of people who get a terminal cancer diagnosis lose their spouses somewhere along the way. Richard let me know from the beginning and many times since, "I'm not going anywhere." He has not missed any of my appointments and has never, ever complained about the inconveniences of this nightmare. We have laughed a lot – more in the beginning than now – but I attribute the laughter to him, not to me. He has always been a happy-go-lucky fellow. Me: the realist. If there is something wrong, I can find it, but he will always remind me of the other side. He loves people, and is energized by time spent with them, while I am drained by too many people or too much time spent in the company of others. This contrast in personality actually works well for us as a couple, but it has also caused occasional angst. For the first few years of my illness, I always let him answer the phone when we returned from an appointment, and he always told folks I was doing well. But I wasn't doing well! We often heard different words from the doctors. And so I would have to "clear things up" at a later date when I talked with my daughters and others who called.

Another interesting thing was happening. For four years, I'd encouraged my husband to attend a support group for caregivers. Of course, being a man, he "didn't need to do that." He was fine. And yet I could see his anger surface from time to time because he wanted "to fix it." So finally, after four years I suggested that I knew he didn't need to go, but would he just go – for me? And he did, and God was involved again. His group wasn't at all what he'd envisioned: just a bunch of women sitting around. There were four men there: a pilot, an interventionist, a high-ranking corporate executive, and Rich – all wanting "to fix it." He now sees himself in others and hasn't missed a meeting in three years. It has been a help to him, coming to grips with the situation, and a help to me, because he truly understands better.

So we have laughed and we have cried, together and separately, supported by each other.

Over time I have worked silently to teach him how to run a household, taking comfort in the knowledge that he will be able to do it in my absence. He has done the marketing for over five years now, and I haven't set foot in a grocery store. He shops for gifts we need. I have gently suggested occasional returns and re-dos, and we do fine with my ideas and his legwork. He willingly takes me places I need to go, and is endlessly patient. It astounds me sometimes. He actually listens to me and changes what he needs to change. Throughout this whole journey, he has been by my side and we are closer than we've ever been. This is my blessing.

———

I have always been somewhat of a loner. Maybe that is not the correct term; I simply enjoy my own company. I am energized by quiet. My husband describes me as "independent." I have always been independent, which comes from the fact that I have had to have a can-do attitude toward life. I left home, technically, at age 17. Can you imagine your children leaving home at that age? I certainly can't. My parents moved to Texas and I stayed in Pennsylvania after high school. I had no job and nowhere to live, but I figured it out. I wanted to attend Drexel University in Philadelphia, so I worked for a year while renting a single room with a shared bathroom down the hall in the home of a very nice older couple. I entered beauty pageants for the money they offered – and I won! So I was able to go to Drexel the following year. There were a lot of obstacles to overcome and challenges to face, for example, not having a car. I literally walked everywhere. I remember washing my face, my clothes, and my few little dishes, all in the same tiny sink in my room. Sometimes my tears fell into the water, too, because I was so lonely. I had no one in my life at that time – even my parents were MIA.

Perhaps my life growing up was a lot different from most. My father was a great salesman. He sold cars to dealerships in the territory he was assigned. The only problem came from the many promises that were made – and broken – by the auto companies. He would bring his territory up to #1 in the country, but the promised rewards were never there. So he'd move on to another company and more promises. The results were always the same. We moved so often my head spins when I try to remember. I became so discouraged that I'd avoid making friends, knowing I'd just have to give them up with the next move. New school. New Friends. Move. Repeat. I remember finally making a conscious decision not to make good friends; it hurt too much to give them up. I kept that vow until we moved to Memphis and I met Donna Roberts. She and I stayed best friends until I was in my 20's. But leaving her cemented my earlier decision; I just couldn't bear to be vulnerable to the pain again.

The positive result that I received from these experiences is a certain resilience, a self-sufficiency that has served me well. I can walk with confidence into any situation, assess it quickly, and talk to anyone. I am not intimidated by anyone's profession, education, or standing in life. I look instead to their character, and for the most part, I listen, rather than talk. This approach has worked well for me, but the result is, admittedly, a lack of close friends. A multitude of acquaintances, yes, and among them many great people, but no best friends. It turns out that my family are the closest people to me, and my best friend is my husband.

One memory that has stayed with me about the room I rented that first year in Philadelphia: on the same floor there was another rented room, occupied by an 86-year-old woman who loved Lawrence Welk. On Saturday nights, I'd invite her over to watch the Lawrence Welk Show on my tiny black-and-white TV. It was all she had to look forward to, and sharing it with her made me happy, too.

Little did I know that sometime much later in life the lessons I learned back then would give me the strength to face lung cancer and a multitude of rigorous treatments. I do have tremendous strength and the will to live, which those around me claim they don't have. I think differently; I believe that each of us has strength beyond what we know, and would be able to call on that strength in a life-or-death scenario. That is the way God made human beings in his image – just look at the pain and suffering Jesus endured.

We are all molded and grow because of our challenges, because of the harder parts of life – not the easy, comfortable times.

I am reminded of what Christopher Robin said to Pooh:

You are stronger than you seem
You are braver than you believe and
You are smarter than you think.

Without realizing it, I am also somewhat of a perfectionist. I've had to relax my standards because I have to depend, now, on others. This is very hard for me because people disappoint me and have throughout my life. I think: if I can do it, I will, because then I'll know it was done right. As I have lost some of my facility and ease in doing things for myself, I've had to accept help from others. I'm learning to keep my mouth shut and accept with grace what others have done for me. I recognize these are gifts and I am grateful for them. I've also learned that the person doing something for me has a happy heart for helping a friend or loved one. Why would I take that away from them? Maybe I am just getting older, as many of my doctors suggest.

———

Purpose

I am always wondering what my purpose is – why am I here? And, why am I still here? I think everyone wonders this, especially as we grow older. And why do we look for or think that our purpose has to be big and bombastic, so the whole world will know? I have no answers for any of these questions; they remain questions. Sometimes I think my purpose was to give birth to two beautiful daughters who in many ways carry me and my values forward: family first; be kind to others, etc. You know all that. But then I think: that can't be it. That was almost 50 years ago.

Surely I wasn't put here to suffer. That would be ridiculous, now wouldn't it?

One of the hardest parts of this journey is losing your life, little by little. It's the little things, like having no stamina, and learning that I don't get "another wind" or a "second wind" – once I use up my strength, I have to rest to restore it. Then I can go on, at a much slower pace, I might add. As I continue to lose things, other things come more into focus. People – other people – each made by God and a part of his wonderful creation. I marvel at that. I enjoy being in the moment with others, when the spotlight is not on me. I love my family more and more for who they are.

I love this passage from II Corinthians. 4.16-18:

> *Therefore do not lose heart, though outwardly we are wasting away, yet inwardly we are being renewed day by day. For our light and momentary troubles are achieving for us an eternal glory that far outweighs them all. So we fix our eyes not on what is seen, but what is unseen, since what is seen is temporary, but what is unseen is eternal.*

Side Effects

It is March 2017 and I am in my 8th month of no treatments. I have done scans every two months, and met with my oncologist, and now I'm waiting. Waiting for the next shoe to drop, so to speak. You would think I'd welcome having the time to enjoy my life – the time to kick back and not worry. But at this point, I am so fragile, I feel like I might break into a thousand pieces. I am not sure where my breaking point is, but it seems mighty close. Why?

Remember all of the treatments: chemotherapy, radiation (three different kinds), immune therapy? Each has left me with side effects, one on top of the other. They don't go away. How much can one person endure? For instance, right now, I am waiting for a heart monitor to arrive so I can wear it for as long as my cardiologist decrees. I dread it – one more thing. My heart began experiencing atrial fibrillation after my surgery. That was 2010. It got worse every time I had chemo. I am now taking four different medications for my heart, including things I said I would never take – for example, blood thinners. Approximately two years ago I had an ablution, and I was good until last Friday. I had an attack that woke me out of a deep sleep – and voila! – my heart is out of rhythm again.

At the end of 2010 we took a trip to California, and the day after I arrived home, I was diagnosed with shingles. My immune system was still down after my surgeries – and voila! – shingles. I endured the pain, thinking it would go away, and I'd be back to normal, or at least my "new normal." For 1% of people who get shingles, the pain doesn't go away – the rash goes, but the pain continues. The virus gets attached to a nerve and stays there for two months, six months, perhaps longer. Perhaps indefinitely. I'm in that 1%. It's now 2017, and I still have the nerve pain, so add another medication.

Fatigue has been with me for the entire journey. I hear that it dissipates for some people. I'm not one of them. So I nap every day. It seems that when I've used up my energy, I have to sleep to regain it. Even when I work out, when the energy is gone, it's gone. I remember that I used to get energy from exercise. Not any more.

"Chemo brain" is terrible for someone like me. My mind is always active; I get ideas all the time. My physical limitations affect my mental productivity. Oh, my. I have arthritis in my lower back, so 3-4 hours, sometime only 2 hours, and I am done in, never to get to any of my ideas. I have never fully recovered from this malady and I feel so stupid when I am unable to put a sentence together. I hear most folks recover from this. I haven't.

One form of radiation I had was proton therapy. It was directed at the tumor, which was once again growing in my right lung (or what was left of it). The therapy did seem to work, but it also did some damage. The very day I finished proton therapy, I began coughing. It was annoying, and I asked my radiation oncologist about it. He said, "Oh, it's common and will go away in 2-4 months." When I got no relief from the cough after many months, I was referred to a pulmonologist to see what he could do to help me. Several tests and scans determined that the radiation had caused scar tissue to form in the airways to the lung, causing it to collapse. I am still coughing, and taking medication for it.

Then of course came immunotherapy, and it was said to be the treatment to beat all treatments. And it worked – it bought me another year. It also bought me RA (Rheumatoid Arthritis) in my hands and feet, as well as an incessant itching on my back and neck, and, quite frankly, wherever it wants to itch. These are autoimmune diseases that ebb and flow but never go away.

Last, but not least, for sure, is cancer pain. Oh, I have never experienced pain like this. The remedy? You guessed it – more pills. Not innocent meds, but opioids and morphine – yes – addictive stuff. I do not wish to become addicted. It scares me. I scared myself so much, I stopped taking them, and then – WOW! – the pain was more than I could stand. So, I take my chances with the drugs.

Every day I wake up wondering which of these "side effects" will get the most attention today. Remember: I can't go on. I go on. Perhaps this sounds like a pity party, and I want to assure you, I don't attend pity parties. They are not much fun, because no one else shows up. I avoid these invitations, but they are coming fast and furious these days. I have been thinking of rolling up the sidewalks and calling it a life. I mean, I don't believe God wants us to just be here to suffer.

———

Last fall, we placed a rather large container outside for the winter. It had housed a plant that had died. Little did we know it also was filled with daffodil bulbs. This March, a warmer month than usual, the flowers began to grow. We were so pleased – almost every day, a new and beautiful bloom appeared. Yet, as each flower fulfilled its purpose, it began to bend back toward the soil from which it had sprung. That bending from the splendor of its height seems to me an apt metaphor for life. Life is beautiful but also fragile. Like the neck of each daffodil as it bent and died, so do we reach up, after a long winter, toward the light, only to bend to earth again, as our glory is spent.

———

It is spring, 2017, and nothing has changed, but everything is different now. I am facing death and no one has to tell me. I have continually lost weight for several months now. I am in constant pain. The fatigue is always there by 2 or 3 o'clock every afternoon. I have been out of treatment for nine months now. I have been told that we will have to start treatment at some point, but they are trying to give me "quality of life." I wonder if they would think this is quality of life if they were living it?

And I recognize freedom. Freedom is now my decision and it is the grace to say, "Yes," and, most importantly, the right to say, "No." I can accept treatment or turn it down. My cancer is slow-growing, so it doesn't appear to change much every two months when I have a PET scan, but, looked at over time, there has been substantial change. I just haven't had the guts to say no or yes. It seems that at the very heart of life, hope beats, the pulse of possibility, even when I know they cannot cure me. It feels like I am the balloon but I also hold the string, and I want so badly to give the string to someone else. But I am reminded that God is with me everywhere I turn.

———

It would not be possible to exaggerate the importance that hymns and songs of faith have played in my spiritual growth. I have learned scripture through song. For over 40 years, I have sung in my church choir, so how could I not remember Joseph Scriven's "Oh, what peace we often forfeit/Oh, what needless pain we bear/all because we do not carry/everything to God in prayer." And my favorite, "Holy, Holy, Holy," brings tears to my eyes every time I sing it, or now, hear it sung. It is big, it is bombastic, and it is the epitome of Praise. We are to Praise God every day. And I wouldn't want to forget my husband's favorite, "Amazing Grace." How that stirs his soul! He always cries through that one. Somehow, he identifies with John Newton as he writes: "I once was lost, but now am found."

———

Happy Memories

It all started more than 25 years ago when we purchased a

time-share apartment in New York City – a great location just a couple of blocks from Central Park and catty-corner from Carnegie Hall. We began going as a family for weekends of shopping and dining in wonderful restaurants. Later, we introduced the "girls' weekend" – so much fun and laughter – although there were also some poignant moments after 9/11. Generally, we were there for a few days of feminine bonding: we shopped, had high tea, ate in Little Italy, took limos, saw many Broadway shows, and always ended our stay with a service at Fifth Avenue Presbyterian Church. We each loved these times, and oh, the memories! When granddaughters reached the age of 12, we began inviting them. Amanda, Jenifer's eldest, was first; we have pictures of her all dressed up in the tackiest clothes. What a hoot! And all of us trying on my wig and laughing. I remember once Denise set her phone to go off in the middle of the night with dogs barking and a rendition of "Who Let the Dogs Out?" – she had hidden the phone under Amanda's pillow!

These hilarious, just-us-girls incidents are forever etched in my mind. However, as I became sicker, we sometimes changed the venue to Spring Lake, New Jersey: the beach, and yes, more shopping, and more great restaurants, but just a little lower key than the city. It was becoming evident as the years went on that I could do less and less. Another time we planned a trip to a Bed & Breakfast in St. Michael's Maryland, which was fine – still good shopping and restaurants. But I wasn't feeling well, and I never knew in advance what shape I'd be in by the time I got there.

So, this year, they planned our "girls' weekend" here in Philadelphia so I could sleep in my own bed at night, and even catch a nap in the afternoons. It was so kind of them to make this all about me. I was very touched. And we did have fun, but I do know it wasn't the same. Although Denise and her daughter, Marta, were away from their Connecticut home, Jenifer, living closer by, was still in family mode – it is hard to truly get away when you keep checking in at home. Still, they did everything for me so we could have another "girls' weekend." I love them all for their thoughts and actions, their time and energy, and their love of those times and memories. It has been a special run of "girls' weekends."

One thing about this most recent weekend that saddened me: Sunday morning. Richard let me sleep in, thinking I was exhausted from the previous day, and not realizing that our tradition had always been to end our weekends in church. Well, they all went to my church and I was missing. I felt so bad; I could have stretched myself and made it to church that morning, but I didn't. Making matters worse: Jenifer's two sons were altar boys at their church that morning, and she missed that to be with me. I hope I have the opportunity to make that right sometime.

Don't cry because it is over. Smile because it happened.
– Dr. Seuss

———

More Hope

Embrace your feelings, experience them, and then release them to prepare your heart for what is to come.

It is still 2017, although I feel as though it should be 2018 because so much has changed for us in such a short period of time. After a year off treatment, I was started on my second immunotherapy drug. After several treatments, my next scan – you know the routine by now. This was a shock! Not only was the new drug not working, but now my cancer had spread to two areas outside my lungs. For eight years, it had stayed in the lungs, but now, it had moved on, to capture more of me.

The next news I received was that the only thing available to me was chemotherapy. This after I had been saying for more than three years that I would never do chemo again. Never, never again! But the human mind has been bestowed with the tremendous gift of forgetfulness. You know: "How bad could it have been? I'm still here and it did work." So, how could I not try it one more time? What if it worked this time? I had to try.

For the next week, I tried not to think about it. My oncologist said that this was the least strong chemo of all chemos – it would be easy. Since I was trying not to think about it, I never considered the fact that I was weaker than I'd been three years ago; that I now weighed at least 25 pounds less than I did three years ago; that I have now been fighting this ugly disease for 8 years. I am tired. I look okay on the outside, so I must be good on the inside. I know that others looking at me only see the good. They still can't see my pain.

Off I go to my first scheduled treatment of new, "easy" chemo. I joke and laugh with my nurses and act like this is a piece of cake. I am once again hopeful. Treatment was on a Monday. On Tuesday I was not feeling well, and each day of the week brought new side effects. We were literally checking off the side effects that "could" happen but "never do." By Saturday, we were in the emergency room. I was scared; I couldn't breathe. Apparently, I had an adverse reaction to this drug of choice, signaling the end of treatments as I've known them.

Sitting in my doctor's office a week later, I knew what I had to hear. My husband was there, and Denise, my elder daughter. I'm not sure just how much one hears and really processes – I was in shock again. As my doctor signed me up for hospice care, he wanted me to give him a hug as I was leaving. But he didn't actually tell me he was signing me up for hospice; he said "palliative" care. So, once again, a small amount of hope flickered. I thought: I can carry on for some time in palliative care. But when the nurse arrived at my house, I was shocked again. She showed me that while the doctor said "palliative' he had written "hospice." To me, they were not at all the same. I am tired. I am in pain. I am dealing with anxiety, which makes me more tired. Here I am again in this vicious circle: which malady will demand my attention today?

I am not depressed. My sense of humor is intact, creating laughter throughout the day. I sleep well and get rest. And even though I know I have maybe six months – more or less – to live, I am still hopeful for many things. First, I am hopeful that my family will finally find peace. What a roller coaster ride this has been for them! I have often felt this is not fair to them. I have often wanted it to be over for them (not to mention me). They have been there every step of the way, never wavering in their commitment to me. How could I not try everything?

I am hopeful that I can leave my life in order – this is so much a part of me. I am working to leave things as easy as possible for others to pick up and carry on. Although her affairs were a bit simpler than mine, my mother did this for me, and I thanked her over and over for her thoughtful care of me. She never heard me, but then, I didn't hear her much in my life, either. My mom was pretty quiet and simply lived by example. I think I always got her messages, although sometimes maybe a year or two later. But when I think about it now, when I finally did get her messages, it was me discovering, and a heck of a good way to learn it, because it was mine. I don't remember her telling anyone how they should live, or think, or dress, or anything. She was a quiet soul, but a deep one. I miss her terribly, still. I just passed on one of her sayings to my granddaughter, and I hope she takes heed: "When in doubt, don't." That kept me safe so many times!

One of my biggest hopes is to be reunited with my mother. I want to hand her a red flower. For the last 18 years of her life, she lived near us, and came frequently for dinners and special occasions. In the spring, when we'd be planting our impatiens for summer and fall color, not one year passed without her suggesting that we include red with our pink and white color choices. We never did. The year my mother died – she died in July – long after planting time had taken place, one single red flower appeared amidst the pachysandra – standing up so proud and tall. That would be my mother.

I am feeling overwhelmed with many emotions. Sometimes I am sad. Sad about what I know must take place. I am scared – not scared of dying, because my final hope is to be in beautiful heaven with God – but I am scared of how I will die.

———

October 2017

Already a month has passed since signing up for hospice. I am getting some things done. Slowly. Very slowly. And I think of more things I need to do, all the while letting go of items on my checklist. One big item was to clean out my closet, since I can no longer wear a size 8 or 10. I am a size 2 now, or an extra-small. So, I begin this project in earnest, thinking it's the right thing to do. After giving away over 30 suits and piling up my casual pants to go, I walk into my closet and tears begin to flow. I can't bear to see so many empty hangers, so much empty space. I am dying, and it makes me sad. For as ready as I am to leave all this pain and weakness behind, I am also still clinging to those around me. I don't really want to leave them and yet, I know I will.

I also think back to the multitude of experiences we had over the years. We traveled three or four times each year. Many of our trips were earned, so we didn't pay anything to go to Disney World, San Diego, Las Vegas, even Australia. Our trip to Australia was three weeks, all expenses paid, and we received a check for $2500 when we landed for "incidentals." What a whirlwind life – 25 of these trips in all. We also traveled on our own all over the country and to many islands. These were mostly trips with our children as they were growing up. Hawaii was a sailing trip that included almost all of the islands.

When Richard was still working for Sun Oil, he had a two-year stint in China, so, his mother, father, and I flew over to spend some time with him. So many memories blend together; it's hard to recount them all. Except one that stands out vividly: Madame Wong. Madame Wong was Richard's counterpart on the China side, and she carefully escorted us around what we were allowed to see in the country. However, Madame Wong also had a personal agenda; she was interested in a ticket to the United States, and she chose Richard to be her ticket.

Men! They can be so oblivious to the women who set their sights on them. Madame Wong certainly had her sights set on Richard. We'd be walking somewhere, and she would get between us, and with sleight-of-hand, push me away. At dinner, she would always sit between us. Once I asked her what was floating in my soup – I guess you could call it soup – just some weak broth with something floating in it that did not look at all appetizing. Madame Wong proceeded to reach across me with her bare hand, scooped the floating thing out of my soup, and popped it into her own mouth. Disgusting!

The Chinese were not allowed up on the floors where the accommodations for Westerners were nicer unless they were invited. She asked Richard to invite her, and lo and behold – he did. He just didn't buy my assessment of her behavior or her motives, so I chose to go along with them to our room. If he was going to be stupid, I would save him. Off we went, and upon entering our room, I stepped into the bathroom for a moment. Somehow, she managed to lock me in! When I finally freed myself, I found them out on the balcony, side by side. She was determined, but I continued to thwart her ways, to save my husband from his too-trusting self.

Travel was a big part of our life, and I can say without reservation that I have no regrets. Perhaps I had my fill, but I am now very content to stay at home. Home is my safe place, my refuge. If I need to sit down or rest, I am free to do just that. I love quiet, and my home is quiet and peaceful. I am presently trying to work on keeping my anxiety at bay, so this environment is very conducive to that. I am anxious about so many things – the things I can no longer do. Simple things, really, but I obviously moved at quite a fast pace all my life, and now when I forget, I begin to pace again – only to find myself coughing, out of breath, and yes, anxious! We don't observe ourselves as we live, but now I must.

———

One Last Hope

"Jesus Wept." (John. 11.35) This may be the shortest verse in the Bible, but it speaks volumes to me. Jesus felt our sorrows and he wept. Just as he sees my suffering and weeps with me. How wonderful to know that he loves me.

I am shocked again! My brother Joe was just diagnosed with AML leukemia. How do you ever wrap your head around this? I am rocked to the core all over again. It is because I know too much about this ugly disease, cancer in any form. I know what he faces and yet I don't say a word. Maybe it will be better for him, so I wouldn't begin to give him advice about chemo. I just feel it in the very core of my being and I dread it for him. He's a babe in the woods right now, and I wouldn't take away even one day of his naïveté. I don't know if he has faith; that is what has sustained me. Maybe it's time to call on my Uncle Johnny. He was the one who brought my father to be a believer, albeit in his 80's.

Jesus weeps.

I am able to do less and less on each passing day. The pain has increased, but when my nurse increases the morphine, I feel too weird, mentally. So I go back to the old dose. More pain, yes. But I can think. I surmise that thinking is more important to me than reducing pain. You really do learn a lot about yourself. Wanting to know is paramount to me – even to the extent that I would like to have blood work done, to see what is happening. But there is no one to order more blood work, and even if there was information there – to what end? Oh, all these questions.

And then I look at my calendar and I laugh. I still put everything on my calendar that I am signed up for or scheduled to do. Then, when the day comes, I must cancel, bow out, say no. What is this all about? I am not ready to become a non-entity, one would assume. I will become a silent voice at my book club, but I will still read the books to maintain a link, however tenuous, to the group of women I have come to know and care about.

The well-wishers. I never knew this would happen, but it has. Everyone wants to come and visit, and I know it is kind of them. I know that, but, honestly, I feel like I'm on display, and 25 pounds skinnier. I love my books, my quiet time, my naps, my writing. (Yes, I said writing!) You see, going out to lunch is too much, and they all want to "do" lunch. Driving there, eating, digesting food – all these simple things that we don't even think about – use energy. And if I spend the required energy, I worry that I won't have enough left to get home. Some of these folks I haven't seen for two years or more. I have a long list now, and am wondering why I need to entertain them. Why don't I just say no? Something I may need to come to grips with along the way.

Just had an "aha!" moment. The more I withdraw from the world, the closer I get to God. "He will cover you with his feathers, and under his wings you will find refuge." (Psalm. 91.4-5) Life's battles will become blessings.

My nurse comes every week, and he is very calming, laid back, listens to me, takes my vitals, and adjusts my medication. His name is Ben. At first, I wasn't sure I wanted a male nurse, but we let it play out and we're glad we did. It took me a while to get him on my side with medications, but now he knows I don't like all the pills I take and I react adversely to many drugs. Anxiety medications make me anxious. Anti-depressants make me depressed. He gets that now, so we are on the same page. I am my own worst enemy when it comes to anxiety. All the time I am reminding myself to relax my shoulders, take a deep breath, and realize I am okay. It's the future I think about all the time and I get anxious. I have to keep bringing myself back to the present moment. Each moment is a gift, and I need to enjoy each one.

Ben told me this week that I am his only patient who is not in bed. I am up and doing until about 2 PM, and then I must nap, but I am grateful for my mornings.

Back to the well-wishers. I learned very quickly not to tell people that I am in hospice. We have friends of forty years' standing who live about an hour and a half away. We haven't seen them in two years. She innocently sent me an email asking me to come for lunch because they are moving to Florida. Since she doesn't know anyone we know, I thought it would be okay to tell her I was under hospice care and couldn't make the trip. Well, an email came back immediately: "OMG. We must come to your hospice place and see you." So I explained that when hospice first started, it meant you only had two or three days left. Today, people stay in hospice care for months, are sometimes released, and may later go back. Once I realized the connotation the term has for many people, only family members were told. Others think I am just out of treatment for the time being.

November 2017

I am relishing every day and it is November! It has been 70 degrees almost every day so it kind of snuck up on me. But today, it's in the 50's, with a lot of leaves still on the trees. Green leaves, in November? We have a little color this year, some yellows and golds, but no striking reds like in years past. We do have lots of fallen leaves, so the task of removing them has fallen on Richard's shoulders. One more thing for him to do. I used to do my part, and I feel sad that I am unable to pitch in. I have limited breath when I am active, in any way, so that curtails my jumping in to help. I still do what I can, albeit very slowly. I am sleeping more these days; it's what I think of all the time. I find myself closing my eyes often, and off to sleep I go. Mornings are my energy times, so I make myself be productive in some way then.

Lunch out with our friends was lovely. They are dear people who actually made it fun. I laughed a lot (haven't done that in awhile). They let me control the time so we were together for almost two hours, and it was okay. Home in time for my nap. I was so glad I did it, after all of my needless anxiety. So glad!

Anxiety is my worst enemy, according to my nurse. If I could control it, I might live a lot longer. Anxiety suppresses the immune system – not a good thing for me. But it is such a way of life for me, I don't always recognize it until my hands are shaking or my shoulders are up and tense. If only there was a natural way of relieving it.

———

November 2017 Continued

My brother is doing well. He seems to have tolerated the massive doses of chemo and transfusions so far. I may have suffered more from my memories of chemo than he did from chemo itself. But he still has a long way to go. And I will recover too. This is Week Two for him since they killed his immune system and no signs yet of its coming back.

Time lapses. Week Three and he is responding positively. Hoorah!

I do a lot of writing in my mind, thinking I'll remember it all, but I don't. So, when I sit down with pen and paper – again – I have none of the wonderful thoughts that I was so sure were worth sharing. I wonder if this occurs with all writers. Am I now a writer? (Editor's note: Yes it does, and yes, you are.)

Life carries on, day in and day out. I do not go out any more; I have no energy and my breathing is more compromised. I use oxygen to sleep now, 12 of the 24 hours we are given. My cancer is slow growing, so this could be a long while, just slowly, ever so slowly declining. My nurse told me this week that with lung cancer, there is no way of knowing the pace of decline. Some people are diagnosed and are gone in a week, or two months. Others linger on and then almost overnight, everything changes, and you go downhill fast, in a matter of weeks, or days, you are gone. This is all hard to think about, to come to grips with. I would only imagine that I'm not the first to go through this, so I always say to myself: If someone else had to do this, I can too. That's how I got through all my surgeries, chemo and radiation treatments, etc. I can do this, too, with a happy heart and good words for others. I have said many times: "I can't go on." I go on.

I may feel helpless but I am never hopeless. As Oliver Sachs said: "I am now face to face with dying, but I am not yet finished with living."

Thanksgiving was hard. We cooked our own dinner, which was a disaster. Gravy was terrible, turkey very tough. Stuffing made with packaged bread cubes was not the same. But most of all, we hurried through it because all my kids, spouses and grandkids plus Richard's brother Michael all came for dessert. Jenifer was stressed, feeling that as soon as they came they should have been leaving. They really don't know how to deal with my end of life. When they left, I slept for 11 hours. I was completely exhausted. Worry besets my next round of holidays. I am getting weaker. Doing the simplest tasks makes it hard to breathe. Oh my.

———

December 2017

Have you ever seen those pictures of the women who survived the holocaust? When I undress and look in the mirror, I see my head superimposed on one of those emaciated bodies. It is so hard to see yourself that way, but it is what it is. I have no fat anywhere, and my muscles are gone – the muscles I worked so hard to maintain for years at the gym. This disease erases all of that, and you are left with – well, not much. It is pitiful, and when dressed, I still look skinny, but I do my hair and put on some make-up, and everyone seems to think I look good. Would they tell me otherwise? I think not.

The good news is, my brother is in remission and gets to go home for 10 days. It's been a journey for sure, only to be continued. If you've had cancer, you will remember after your treatment, you were warned of rogue cells lurking somewhere, and so you "should" have chemo – or further chemo – to be sure they have gotten everything. So my brother and his wife will return to Seattle for round 2, a repeat of round 1. There is a round 3 and a round 4, but we get ahead of ourselves. They will be missing Christmas, just as they missed Thanksgiving, with their daughter. It is a tough road ahead, but he did respond, and at this point, no leukemia cells are presenting themselves.

———

It's a simple thing, changing the calendar every day. I have used the same wooden calendar in my kitchen for probably 10 years or more. This small act went unnoticed until the last month or so. Now I notice it. I thank God for each and every day he gives me here on planet Earth, among my family and a few good friends. I miss my extended family, but I have no way of being around them now.

Getting ready for Christmas has its challenges. Cards are done – Hallelujah! Took me a week. Now it's wrapping, with help – lots of help! Then, on to decorating, which is all up to Richard. I won't be hauling things here and there, standing and reaching up to decorate the tree. We never even thought of these simple things when it was easy. And maybe, just maybe, I seem to only be thinking of the simplest things.

I do not want my life defined by the disease I have had for the past 8 years; I don't want it to eclipse, erase, overshadow the first 62 years. What did I do then? I came across a good description of who I think I am in Hebrews. 11.1: "Faith is being sure of what we hope for and certain of what we do not see."

Life has become smaller and smaller. We went to visit friends in their new, "assisted living" apartment. Oh my, I am glad I will never do that! They made it all very easy and simple for me, and yet, I paid the price of increased pain for two days afterwards, I think from just being overtired. Too small, my world.

The next big challenge is Christmas. Denise and Spencer will come for two nights and Christmas Day. Entertaining is not in my DNA any more. I am really not sure how I will fare, but their daughter Amanda is in a special school in Arizona, and it is a sad time for them, so of course, I didn't want them to be alone. What kind of Christmas cheer will I bring?

How much can change in a short year? My daughter Jenifer is recovering from rotator cuff surgery; my brother Joe returns to Seattle for round 2 of chemo; granddaughter Marta is away at school; and here I sit, unable to provide much support to anyone. I hope and pray that all other family members will enjoy family and friends in their usual fashion.

———

Big Changes

In mid-December, I was doing a perfectly normal thing – heading into the bathroom. The next thing I remember is looking up at the ceiling and wondering what happened. I had passed out – doing some damage to my body in the resulting fall. Six days later, I am still trying to recover, but it saddens me, and rocks me to my core. My heart is going into a-fib, and although I am taking medication (another one, yes) it happened again. This time I could get to my bed without passing out. But I wonder: will I never go out again?

I had big plans for December. I wanted to attend a cantata at church, the final Session meeting to complete my term, and Christmas Eve services. Like all of my calendar plans, I am not attending. I am canceling. So, as I see it, I will not put any more of my wish list on the calendar for January. What will become of me? I wonder how many others ponder that question. Surely I'm not the only one. I love the prayer of St. Francis of Assisi, especially the ending, "Grant that I may not so much seek to be consoled, as to console, to be understood as to understand, to be loved, as to love. For it is in giving that we receive, it is in pardoning that we are pardoned, and it is in dying that we are born to eternal life." I have always remembered this when dealing with others. But now, where are the others?

I have my family and for that I am blessed. Life is good. Christmas is this week and we will see our family in stages. They are so kind to respect my limitations and work their hectic schedules around me. How did I ever deserve all of this?

My brother has completed round 2 of his chemo. Seven hours every day for 5 days. Now it's on to transfusions to bring him back. He is stronger this time, but nonetheless, you wonder how much the body can take. He is 72, after all. I pray that he is comfortable and peaceful. I don't want to transfer any of my suffering to him so our text messages are always upbeat. I wonder if our parents are looking down on us?

December 27

I actually made it through Christmas! I wasn't holding out much hope. The feeling remains of watching from afar. If I were a piece of meat, I would be overdone. Feelings are real, but mine are strange. We welcomed everyone, but I really didn't take part in much. Physically, I'm present, but mentally, not so much. Jenifer and Amanda both cry and hold me tight. They are not in a good place emotionally. Have to get them some help. They are missing out on spending their time with me. Denise is very stoic. I am absent mentally and, I suppose, emotionally. My pain just takes over and it is hard to engage. We must move past all this so we can enjoy each other, maybe like we used to? Or will this be the new normal, too? I am still hoping.

My one last hope is that life is eternal. Yes, I believe it so, and because of my faith, I have made it so far. I wake each morning with a list of things I am going to do. Do I do them? No, not all, because I run out of energy, or my pain is too bad, but hopeful is how I start each day. I do love my mind, a gift from God. It is still in high gear most days, and I have learned to accept my limitations and not be angry with myself. I do love people who can engage with me, and make me think and talk, while putting away all the small talk. Small talk wears me out.

May the God of Hope fill you with all joy and peace in believing, so that by the power of the Holy Spirit, you may abound in Hope. (Romans. 15.13)

I am experiencing incredible pain in my right hip and lower back, so that I am hardly able to walk. So, we tried another medication – yes, another one – to alleviate this pain. Well, back to square one, because I simply couldn't stay awake, no matter what. I tried to do things, only to find myself sitting down and immediately going to sleep. I do remember what I wrote earlier: I would rather have the pain than not be able to think. But this pain may be the end. Since the cancer has spread to my adrenal glands, I am thinking this is cancer pain. It doesn't go away.

New Year's Eve is approaching. Amazing. And now people want to visit again. There's Pam, Jenifer and Amanda, my pastor. Makes me crazy. I get it from their standpoint. They want to see me. What's left of me. Jenifer and Amanda are most welcome any time. They get it. Actually, my pastor also gets it, I guess. I just worry about Pam. Anyway, I will weather this, too.

So I found out about this most recent painkiller. Although it is topical, it goes in and kills the pain (and your brain). They use this drug before and after surgery because they don't want you to remember the surgery at all. This is a mind-altering drug, and it sure altered mine. What a horrible feeling. I couldn't put a sentence together. It was scary. But as soon as I washed it off: Back to Me.

January 2018

I feel like I am writing my diary. Boring! And it may very well be, because I feel like this has got to be near the end, somehow. The pain is overwhelming me. I cannot do anything physical because I am unable to move. I try to read, to write, do computer things, but I just fall asleep. I am sleeping way too many hours, but then wake up around 5 AM, very anxious. At 7, the pills start: 7, 8, 9 AM, so I am up or re-setting my alarm clock. What life is this?

Lots of snow and frigid weather. Since I don't go out anyway, why can't I just enjoy the pretty snowfall in the security of my home? I think it makes me feel trapped.

My brother is still in Seattle for at least another couple of weeks. He is getting platelets and transfusions and is doing well. He never lost his hair – one lucky guy!

I don't want this to be all about me, so I will say: Pam is not coming. She was very gracious when Richard called her. It raises my anxiety level when anyone is coming. However, I do need people, so Jenifer is coming tomorrow. With her, I won't feel as though I am on display or have to explain anything.

Another day. The pain is incredible. I have put on every pain killing cream I have except the one that makes me mentally unstable. So I work through the pain. I figure that I will have it no matter what, so why not do the dishes, the laundry? I did my hair for the first time all week and put on some make-up. I feel better when I look better. We all do.

———

Walk With Me
author unknown

If you have learned to walk
A little more sure-footedly than I,
Be patient with my stumbling then
And know that only as I do my best and try
May I attain the goal
For which we both are striving.

If through experience, your soul
Has gained heights which I
As yet in dim-lit vision see,
Hold out your hand and point the way,
Lest from its straightness I should stray,
And walk a mile with me.

———

January 10, 2018

The pain.

Where do I go from here? Maybe close to resolving the issue. I have a doctor's appointment in two days to try to get a better handle on what's happening to me. Hip pain is relentless. Pain in my right side, when it is there, pulls and stabs. When I lost all of my weight, I also lost my breasts (tiny little things for the first time in my life – like no-need-for-a-bra tiny). Well, then they got bigger, which worried me, thinking I was retaining fluid. So, hospice suggested I see my primary doctor; it might be SVC Syndrome. Simply put, the tumor in my chest may have grown and could be leaning on my aorta, hence the swelling. So, the way my mind works, the tumor on my adrenal gland had grown, too, and was causing the pain in my hip. Treatment would be radiation, which I cannot do. Just physically cannot get to radiation appointments. Not to mention the fact that I shouldn't do any further radiation, according to my last radiation oncologist. You feel as though the walls are closing in on you. There is no place to hide.

So, on to my primary physician where I'll probably find out I am all wrong. I forget I have a very slow-growing cancer, and so this pain is probably the result of my fall. Either a pinched nerve or a fracture. The fracture – if there is one – will need to heal on its own. No surgery in my future. Meanwhile, I'm on to steroids for a pinched nerve.

I have had some relief, but not total yet. The mind is amazing – once again I had my tumors the size of a cat and growing. I'll bet all cancer patients imagine far worse than what's really going on.

Fear of the unknown. We all do it – have a pain here or there and we immediately imagine the worst. Our minds are capable of creating things, so I always ask myself, "Is that what you want?" Control that mind – no matter what.

⸺

Family

So wonderful and so curing. Amanda comes to see me and always cries, so we are talking about that. I told her that it is okay to cry because it tells me how much she cares. She is off to college again, so a distance away that worries her. She was just told over the holiday that I am in hospice, so she worries. Marta has finally moved on to Phase 2 at her school! A huge accomplishment for her. I have to write to her more often. I have neglected to write and I'm not sure why.

My grandson Nicholas wanted to come and see me, so he came during the football game and we chatted about that. I think he just wants to see that I am still here. Nothing beyond that. Matthew, his older brother, is stoic, doesn't say much, never asks questions, and doesn't let on where he is with this. I love when they talk to me, but nothing there right now.

Jenifer and Denise seem to be tripping all over themselves to do things for me. Denise came and stayed for several days, and cooked, and brought all kinds of food. Jenifer just worries. I know they mean well, but for someone like me who needs her space – well, I am ready for them to leave when they do. I love them all so much. I have no way to do for them except to let them do for me. That helps them, I understand. We have to let others do for us. That's our way of giving back to them.

Of course, my husband seems to be the rock. He never waivers, does all he can for me every day without complaint. I often wonder why I have this unwavering support. He says he is glad he can do this all for me. Wow! What a man he is. We never know all this when we get married. If you think about it now, when we are in our 70s, who knew it would be like this? I am totally blessed!

January 15

Life is good.

I watch others going and doing – living their active lives every day, and sometimes I wish that I could do more – just simple things I used to do. I remember what it was like to do what you wanted, when you wanted. Most people don't know just how fortunate they are. I certainly was not grateful. I had no idea how life could change on a dime. As I look back, it is like a flash – eight years so far, and yet it seems that everything changed in a moment. And I see that this could happen to anyone. Look at my brother – two months so far in a hospital in another city, away from home. Life put on hold. You wonder, how did that happen? In a flash. I pray every day for health for our entire family and all our friends.

January 17

I came across a poem that got me to thinking about the little things we do that get carried down, generation after generation, having the greatest impact far beyond what we can imagine. I know that Richard's mother read to them all as small children, especially when they were sick and needed to be quiet. Once Richard was in bed for several days with some serious infection, and his mother sat beside him for hours, reading the historical novel, "Below the Salt," from beginning to end. It was summertime, and Jill sat in the doorway of his room, not allowed too close, but listening intently. He was probably 11 or 12, and she no more than 6 or 7. Those experiences instilled a love of reading in all three children: Richard, Michael, and Jill. The poem, "I Had a Mother That Read to Me," is even engraved on their mother's headstone. When our children were small, we read to them every night before bed – a time to quiet and get ready to sleep. Our two girls repeated this with their children, so our grandchildren have the love of reading, too. I am sure that Jill and Michael carried on this tradition with their own children, and now those children read to the next generation as well.

Oh, the love of books.! Your imagination can take you anywhere. And so, down the generations it goes. This one small thing that we never really knew would have such an impact. So, I share with you this poem, so aptly expressed:

> We search the world for truth, we cull
> The good, the true, the beautiful,
> From graven stone and written scroll,
> And all old flower-fields of the soul;
> And, weary seekers of the best,
> We come back laden from our quest,
> To find that all the sages said
> Is in the Book our mothers read
> — author unknown

> Our example, our words, our ideas, and our ideals can be projected into the future to live forever in the lives of others. Books bring to life the inspiration of the past.
> — Wilfred A. Peterson

January 20

I have to say, I have had some relief, sometimes for an hour, sometimes for several hours. Prednisone seems to be helping. I just took my last pill this morning and now I'll have to see if there is anything else I can do. When I have no pain. It is so wonderful! So amazing! I feel human; I feel great. And I wish it to last. I think: I could do this. What a difference. Wow!

January 25

Back with a vengeance. Pain!!!
So I had an MRI done on Wednesday, and alas, no pinched

nerve to address with a cortisone shot. No, the pain is from the further spread of cancer. It's now in my bones. And I kind of knew that from hearing others describe bone cancer pain. It is unbearable, and so now is the time to double up on the meds and get some relief. Not sure if I will be writing much more as what I write could be unintelligible. I will try my best, but I do feel weird when I take more medication than I have been.

———

February 15, 2018

I have been waiting to write because I wasn't sure what the ending would be. Now I know. A resident at Penn suggested radiation to my chest to alleviate the fluid build-up that I am experiencing. Let me step back and clarify: I have two major areas to deal with. One is the pain of new tumors in my spine. I had radiation last week and it basically just didn't work. I still had the pain. The second issue is a thoracic tumor that is pressing on my heart, causing me to retain fluids. Again, pain, but in my breasts, which are hard and feel like I need to feed a baby.

I felt, once again, that I was being pushed to do more treatment – treatment that I feel is too hard to do. My radiology oncologist called today and recommended against any further radiation. Too risky – or the risks outweigh the benefits. So, now, we do what I should have been doing all along: making me comfortable. Back to hospice and medications. It feels like a giant weight has been lifted. I don't have to go on.

From my bible study came some "aha" moments: for instance, the difference between faith and trust is action. In allowing others to do things for me, I've put trust in them: taken action. Stepping back is taking action. Interesting how so many of these things are the opposite of what we think they are. Trusting someone else to do something for me – and staying out of it – is very difficult for me. Gosh, at this stage of life, a new challenge to overcome!

This grief thing – I don't believe you get past something like that. You get through it to be healthy. Don't avoid it. Face it.

Wind is breath. The gift of life.

February 25

Every day I have great intentions. I think: today I'll write. Then the pain comes and I simply cannot think.

It dawns on me that my whole focus is to get dressed and cleaned up for the day. Did I ever think about that before? Does anyone? I don't believe I did. I just went through the motions. I was already thinking about my day and what I had planned. Life has been reduced to the very basics. One morning recently, I said to Richard: "I'm going to put on some clothes (no bra), throw water through my hair, and call it a day." How I've changed!

> *Alice laughed. "There's no use trying," she said. "One can't believe impossible things."*
>
> *"I dare say, you haven't had much practice," said the Queen. "When I was your age, I did it for half an hour every day. Why sometimes, I've believed as many as six impossible things before breakfast."*
>
> – Lewis Carroll:
> *Through the Looking Glass*

Sounds like me every morning. I have my list of what I am going to do each day. I believe I can do these things – until I get started, the pain comes, and I am finished. All I really want to do is finish the story.

The Velvet Hammer

I am probably known for saying what is on my mind, and rather bluntly at times. My family calls me "the velvet hammer." To them I say: The only reason I would say anything to one of you that could be taken as hurtful is because I love you. I see something that, if corrected, will give you benefits beyond your knowing. And, if left to go down the path you are on, I can see that you will be hurt over and over again. I am not trying to remake you. I would never do that. I love you the way you are. It's about changing some thing you are doing, not changing you.

March 1, 2018

At the end of September, I was officially put in the care of hospice. It was mentioned, casually, that the way the disease would normally progress would give me another six months. That brings me to March. How casually I change the kitchen calendar blocks day after day. How casually I live each day, putting up with limitations, wanting to appear normal so as to not scare those around me. I work hard at this. I am a rules person, and I know the rules.

So. I think about this all the time. How could I not? I feel as though I am watching this unfold from somewhere else. Yes, there is the pain; yes, I feel alone. I can't imagine how anyone else could know what this is like. I still do not. It is surreal, even to me.

Many of my cancer "colleagues" have passed on. They have gone before me; they are out of pain. The one common denominator has been that they stopped eating. So I eat, every meal, every day. I figure if I keep eating, I won't die. And yet I am not really living, am I? Does anyone even know this except me? Is that what matters? Women, much more than men, have learned to mask their feelings. In fact, I know women who can look you in the eye with a big, beautiful smile and still be in immense physical or emotional pain. Why did we learn this so well?

Have a heart that never hardens
and a temper that never tires,
and a touch that never hurts.
— Charles Dickens

Somehow, this is what being a woman means to me. Through

my mother, no doubt. Stiff upper lip and all that. Don't complain.

———

March 8

So what happened in the last week? Two major snowstorms struck. A limb went through our car and it had to be towed. Of course, they delivered the car to the wrong shop, so in effect, we lost one car for three days. We had no electricity for five days, but we had a generator for the essentials, like my oxygen. The generator was a gas-guzzler, so Rich was off in horrendous weather, keeping the gas coming so I could breathe. He was exhausted and worried. We cooked outside on the grill. We were actually making it all work. Then the generator died. Yes, just died. We were able to borrow our neighbor's generator, as they were in Washington. What else could go wrong? Well, I won't bore you, but this is how I lose weeks at a time. And don't we all – without realizing it? I am time-conscious in a way, for a reason, that most people are not. Today, the sun is out, there's a beautiful blue sky, and life resumes. For everyone except me. I am stuck in a sort of time capsule, between living and dying – not able to do either one.

———

The Past Does Matter

One of my brother's oncologists asked if he had spent any time in the Ohio River Valley as a child. Well, we did live there for some time in the 1950s, when we were both young. The state was busy building roads and infrastructure, disrupting the soil. There appears to have been a lot of mold stirred up by all this building. The oncology team in Seattle say that this may have been the origin of my brother's leukemia. When I heard this, I recalled a similar conversation with my oncology team, early in my treatment. Taken on its own, one case at a time, few connections are made. But, remember, my dad also had lung cancer. Interesting.

March 11

My mind is so active. I have a list of things to do that would make a healthy person tired. I am slowly, ever so slowly, working through the process of cleaning out old files, sorting through boxes of old pictures, and so on. Every day I get a little more done. I am truly blessed with a mind that still works, although more of the body is shutting down. I am on oxygen all the time because of the thoracic tumor in my chest, which is leaning on my heart and airways. The nerves going to my right leg have been affected by the tumors in my spine, so the leg hurts and feels weak, like it might not support me. There's a creepy feeling of something on my leg when nothing is there. I guess this is a sort of neuropathy. I know that I could end up in a wheelchair and some folks even face amputation. That is not an option for me. Even the wheelchair – oh, my. Saying goodbye is the hardest thing to do. I am saying goodbye to some folks and many things. Will walking be a part of that too? Someone said: "You know that you are in love when the hardest thing to do is say goodbye."

So many thoughts now about so many really important topics. Here's one we all need to give thought to:

Forgiveness is the fragrance that the violet sheds on the heel that has crushed it.
– Mark Twain

The Bible also teaches us that we cannot be healthy if we don't forgive. I have tried to forgive those who have hurt me. I've prayed, asking God to help me forgive, and I've felt a sense of relief when I did. I want to search my memory to be sure I have forgiven everyone. We owe it to each other.

March 15

God is good. I have energy and have accomplished a lot this week.

Being able to clean out your desk at any stage of life feels good. And one whole filing cabinet full of cancer related papers.

Wow! I even may have inspired Rich to do the same – he just has no time because of all he does for me. I don't need as much sleep as I did for awhile. I am eating well – love fruits and vegetables – and homemade chocolate chip cookies! So God is good to me.

The only difficult part of shredding and discarding were the memories. I was a commercial real estate agent; I was a paralegal for 14 years; we had our own business, sometimes simultaneously with our careers. As I sorted and shredded I remembered things that surprised me. Traveling – we were always traveling with our girls. I came across a log book that was written by a group of Girl Scouts we took sailing on the "Brilliant" so that they could get their sailing insignias. We were chaperones and crew on this week-long adventure. All of the girls who entered in the log book wrote how touched they were, knowing we had committed the time and money to be with them. Their own parents were too busy to vacation with them. Things haven't changed much, have they? Too many parents are just too busy for their kids, and believe me, the kids notice. Too many of these children feel as though they are not valuable. So sad.

I am halfway through my sixth month on hospice. The doctors said maybe six months, maybe less. My nurse says I am stable. Hospice is supposed to make you comfortable – that is what they do. I am not there yet. My nurse is off to Kenya to bring 3 children here to live with him and his wife. And he is going to bring them to meet me. What's that about? I do not protest too loudly, though, since I don't want to be dropped from the hospice program because I am doing too well. Then I would have no one to go to in an emergency. That's scary.

March 25

Interesting happenings in my small world this week. Six months has officially come and gone in hospice so I need to be re-certified in order to continue. My meeting with this health professional (a nurse) shed light on how patients with lung cancer die. Since no one really knows for sure, I won't write about it, but I think I know which path my broken body will take. I have worried about this for some time now. It is not a happy ending for me.

Since Ben, my regular nurse, is out of town, I've also been visited by another R.N. They are all really thorough and well-trained. This nurse wants me to be pain-free, and explained how I can achieve that. I never heard this before. Pain free? So, I take my liquid morphine as frequently as every three hours, and keep a log as to how I feel: assessing my pain level as well as my ability to think. Then the doctor can calculate the level of morphine in the pills I take to help me be free of pain. They up the pills and I stop taking the liquid. Easy, right? Not so much. For one thing, constipation accompanies morphine use – probably all opioids – and so does inability to think. Oh, my. But I am doing this – in the midst of it actually on Day 3. See, there is still hope in the midst of all this.

The cancer in my spine is growing quite quickly. I can feel it and see it now. It's what is causing all the pain. The thoracic tumor is growing, too, but I can't see it or feel it in the same way. But it is harder to breathe. I notice that.

So here I am again, trying to figure out how to live my best life. And they will be back – in two months this time – to re-certify me. Wow. Two months rather than six.

We may have done everything we could in our fight against this ugly disease. The word itself creates a barrier between you and your loved ones that never existed before, and you think you can fight it, but cancer doesn't care about effort.

March 27

Going to the dentist yesterday was a downer that I did not anticipate. Everyone in the office has been more than kind to me. I have cancelled appointments several times, but the dentist understands my situation and has tried hard to accommodate me. On more than one occasion, he has come in on a Saturday to see me. The office is closed, of course, but he's been willing to do that. He's also given us his cell phone number so we can call him directly, saying that if I'm having a good day, I should just call and he'll fit me in. All the folks who work for him are in sync with this flexibility.

So, yesterday, everyone gives me a hug, but they don't ask how I am doing. All was quiet around me. So much so, that I was uncomfortable. They know it is probably the last time they will see me; I know it is my last teeth cleaning.

This is all so weird to me. What am I hopeful about? Especially after seeing two new nurses in the past two weeks. Both of these excellent nurses have reminded me that I am dying. I happened to mention addiction and I was told: we don't worry about that; you'll be on morphine for the rest of your life anyway. I wonder why they need to keep telling me? Maybe they think I am in denial. Maybe I am.

Hope. I keep wondering about hope. Is it a want? A need? A desire? That what I want may indeed happen? Can you have hope without faith? Just to believe for one more day, one more hour, maybe, that there is something out there, waiting for me to discover. What would I have without hope? Nothing. What does it take to hope these days? Everything!

April 1

Happy Easter! Yes, Easter is happy!

April 2

I saw my nurse this morning, and he assured me that we could work on my medications to accomplish limited pain but that "no pain" wasn't realistic for me. I had already come to that conclusion. My substitute nurse had adjusted my morphine to such a degree that I was knocked out most of the time. Not for me! I want to be awake and participating in life, limited as it is, as much as I can. So my regular nurse, Ben, is back now and we agree: yes: limited pain, but not "no pain" for me. We continue to work toward that goal.

My daughter Jenifer shared a book with me that explains why God doesn't heal some of us even when he has done so for many others. The book is entitled, When God Doesn't Fix It, by Laura Story. According to this theory, healing would be the lesser thing for some. God uses the stories of those of us who are broken, whose journey has been a mess. In writing this account from the beginning,

I've been asking: "Why am I doing this?" I'm really putting myself out there since I am such a private person, always wanting to appear in control and "as perfect as possible." But God didn't use perfect people. He used the woman at the well; he used David (what a mess his life was). So if he wants to use me, in all my broken-ness, I'll fit right in. God sees the bigger picture. His story is so much bigger than ours. Might he reveal himself to someone through my story? However, keep in mind, it is not about me. I am just the conduit, which is comforting to me.

Blessings
by Laura Story

We pray for blessings, we pray for peace
Comfort for family, protection while we sleep
We pray for healing, for prosperity
We pray for Your mighty hand to ease our suffering
And all the while, You hear each spoken need
Yet love us way too much to give us lesser things

'Cause what if Your blessings come through rain drops
What if Your healing comes through tears
What if a thousand sleepless nights are what it takes to know You're near
What if trials of this life are Your mercies in disguise

We pray for wisdom, Your voice to hear
We cry in anger when we cannot feel You near
We doubt Your goodness, we doubt Your love
As if every promise from Your word is not enough
And all the while, You hear each desperate plea
And long that we'd have faith to believe

'Cause what if Your blessings come through rain drops
What if Your healing comes through tears
What if a thousand sleepless nights are what it takes to know You're near
What if trials of this life are Your mercies in disguise

When friends betray us
When darkness seems to win
We know that pain reminds this heart
That this is not,
This is not our home
It's not our home

'Cause what if Your blessings come through rain drops
What if Your healing comes through tears
What if a thousand sleepless nights are what it takes to know You're near

What if my greatest disappointments or the aching of this life
Is the revealing of a greater thirst this world can't satisfy
What if trials of this life
The rain, the storms, the hardest nights
Are Your mercies in disguise

It is my hope that my family will finally find peace and learn to carry on in productive ways. I feel the need to apologize for the eight-year nightmare I've put them through. They need to know I wish them happiness in their lives – not perfection – just simple, "aha" moments to live by. I also want them to know that if I can, I will ask God to guide their steps.

Psalm 23

The Lord is my shepherd; I shall not want.
He maketh me to lie down in green pastures: he leadeth me beside the still waters.
He restoreth my soul: he leadeth me in the paths of righteousness for his name's sake.
Yea, though I walk through the valley of the shadow of death, I will fear no evil: for thou art with me; thy rod and thy staff they comfort me.
Thou preparest a table before me in the presence of mine enemies: thou anointest my head with oil; my cup runneth over.
Surely goodness and mercy shall follow me all the days of my life: and I will dwell in the house of the Lord for ever.

Interlude

Here is where the "first edition" of Micki's story ended. Six months and more in hospice had elapsed and, given the depredations of her disease, we all – Micki included – felt the end of her life was imminent. I rushed off to Philadelphia with her book, fearing even as the plane left the runway that I'd be too late. Instead, we had a couple of days that felt almost normal – staying up late to talk, and sharing pleasant meals. It was a few moments out of time, a gift I'll always treasure. She was obviously very gravely ill, and in tremendous pain, but somehow she summoned the strength to participate for those few stolen hours.

I returned to Colorado, thinking that the call could come at any time. But days, and then weeks, passed by, and Micki didn't die. Nor did she stop writing. Pleased as she was with the physical form of her journal, she had yet more to say. Writing was a lifeline, and one she would not easily relinquish.

We were all learning that lives do not have a predictable number of chapters. There are second editions, and afterthoughts, and addenda to be lived, and written.

Jenifer Jill Digby Gile
At Liberty
Denver, Colorado
August 2018

Micki's Story, Continued

April 15th

Tax day! I haven't been hearing much this year about tax day – have they changed the date taxes are due? I live in my own self-crafted bubble, and if I don't dwell on it, I am quite happy. Because of my pain, there are no expectations put on me by others. I can run the show if I want to. And sometimes, I admit, I do. I am the gatekeeper, the pill dispenser, the bill payer, the meal planner – all from the comfort (sometimes) of my wing chair. But I can't think about it or I'm afraid I would go down in depression. So I write, I read a lot, and I'm taking an online course on the Holy Spirit. But wait! I am dying. Oh. I feel this disease progressing, so why do I continue to do all these other things? Shouldn't I be putting all my energy into dying? Isn't that what one does in my circumstances? The doctors have already been proved wrong: I passed the six month mark in hospice and I'm still here. The other day I had these thoughts: I am gaining weight. I sleep like a baby. I am interested more in life than in death. Maybe – just maybe – I am getting better. Now, wouldn't that be something? I go full circle and get better. Maybe taxes aren't due on April 15th.

April 17th

Grit and Grace: there is a tension between the two. It takes grit to get up and get dressed every day, working through the pain, but since there is no mention of my pain, I assume it is through grace? I am dying (well, aren't we all?) more every day, and yet, I am very much about living. I'm not sure I'm doing such a great job of living – maybe dying is just what I can do in a limited way. Also, even though I write a lot about dying, I really don't think about it the rest of the time.

How do we learn to die? I, for one, don't know a whole lot about it. Would you know how to do it? Everyone is different and we will all experience this somewhat differently – physically. I get that. But what I am trying to wrap my mind around is this: What should I be thinking? How should I be acting (differently)? How should I be using my limited time? My time has been limited for quite some time now. Nothing has changed. Yet everything has changed.

So, there I go again, being human. I want control, but it doesn't work that way. God knows all and God is in control. Why are we not able to remember that and then leave it there? I mean, he's the one who made us this way. Or is this a result of spending 70 years here on this earth? More opposites. Grit. To get through this life here on planet earth. Grace. To go forward with God.

And God said, "No."
by Claudia Minden Weisz

I asked God to take away my pride,
And God said "No."
He said it was not for Him to take away,
But for me to give it up.
I asked God to make my handicapped child whole
And God said, "No."
He said her spirit is whole, her body only temporary.

I asked God to grant me patience.
And God said, "No."
He said that patience is a by-product of
tribulation. It isn't granted, it's earned.
I asked God to give me happiness,
And God said, "No."
He said he gives blessings. Happiness is up to me.

I asked God to spare me pain.
And God said, "No."
He said, "Suffering draws you apart from worldly
Cares and brings you closer to Me."
I asked God to make my spirit grow,
And God said, "No."
He said I must grow on my own, but He will prune
me to make me fruitful.

I asked God if He loves me,
And God said, "Yes."
He gave His only Son who died for me, and I will
Be in Heaven someday because I believe.
I asked God to help me love others as much as
He loves me,
And God said, "You finally have the idea."

———

April 22nd

When talking with others, if you simply ask a question about them, you can usually sit back and rest while they dominate the conversation. Just a couple of days ago, I asked one leading question of someone who dropped in to see me. An hour and a half later, he was still talking. About different subjects, mind you, but never did he inquire about us. Same scenario with a friend on the phone. She only talked for a half hour because I had to cut it short. But it was all about her. I conclude that others are uncomfortable with anyone who is now "different." I experienced the same thing at the store the other day. We went to a card store, and everyone who helped us in any way spoke only to Richard and not to me. I recognized it pretty quickly and purposefully tried to make eye contact. Didn't happen – and I only had oxygen, no other trappings of the "handicapped." From now on, when I meet anyone head-on who is suffering from an apparent physical challenge, that person will get my attention, not the companion or caregiver. What a great lesson to know how that feels, so I can fix it in me. I hope you fix it in you.'

At the same time, I find myself too self-centered. The pain is there 24/7, reminding me of what I can and can't do. But I still dream of a better life someday. There have been so many folks who have done amazing things for me, one after another. Flowers, gifts, lunch, plants, dinner, videos from Alaska. So I wonder why I don't think of others and do things for them? I am too self-centered. That is what this situation does to you. Break out of it and learn to love others more. This has been on my heart for some time now. I need to change.

When I wake up in the night, I make lists, sometimes for hours. Lists upon lists of all the things I am going to do. Oh, I see myself doing these things, and I have to admit, it's exciting. No wonder I am so tired when I get up in the morning. I am fairly comfortable at night – it must be lying down – but it seems that the rest of the time pain is a constant. I want a pain that has a beginning, a middle, and an end, not one that goes on forever and cuts all the way through to the bone. Literally.

April 27th

I blame it on morphine: my spelling and handwriting are deteriorating. So many people are kind to me, sending me books to read, flowers and cards to enjoy, wreathes for my door: you name it. And I must send thank you notes, but when I write them, I misspell, I cross out – not me. Can I blame it on the morphine? It's also old age, but I don't think of myself as old. Seventy? Is that old? If you are in your 20s or 30s, maybe 70 seems old, but when you get there, it doesn't. What is too young to die? These are all the questions one asks when sitting around, waiting for it to happen. I wonder all the time: is it today? It can't be; I feel the same as I did yesterday, and the day before that. Why do doctors tell you when they think you are going to die? It's not good for the soul.

My brother is on the last day of 25 days of chemo. This has been going on since November. Now, it is wait and see if a stem cell implant will be necessary. He has done well: no hair loss; some weight loss (which he liked); no nausea. Amazing. My prayer is the he is good to go now. Back to life.

———

Grief

Grief is God's gift to us that helps us heal. He never gives you something to deal with without also giving you the means to do so. I know this firsthand as I have experienced the grief process several times in my life. The strongest and most profound memories are from my mother's death. She had been in the ICU for fully three months when she died. I learned later that Medicare limits coverage to exactly that length: three months and no more. But I digress.

For a whole year after my mother's death, I could not attend church. When the organ began, so did my tears, and I would have to leave the service and go home. During that year, two people that I regarded highly sought me out and suggested that I go to grief counseling. You probably know my response to that: "I'm too busy;" "I don't want to talk about it with a bunch of strangers." And on and on. I did, however, know that I was emotionally unhealthy. One knows that in the same way one knows when one is physically unhealthy.

Then I saw an ad in our local newspaper about a grief counseling class that was starting, so I decided to check it out. The first thing that was wrong was the age of the facilitator. She was in her 20s or 30s! Too young, in my opinion, to know anything about grief. I found out later that she had lost her brother in an automobile accident, so she did know something about grief and loss. Oh, how we judge! Every time you attended a session, you told your story and listened while others did the same, much like a meeting of Alcoholics Anonymous. Almost every time I attended, I would drive home thinking: "This is really stupid. I don't need this." But I kept going back for quite some time. Long enough to hear one woman who was angry with her husband for dying. She was so mad at him – and I found this humorous – until I realized that I had once been angry at my mother's doctors. Anger is probably the first step in the process of healing, and I had moved past it. I saw this in myself only because I was seeing it in others. Another instance that comes to mind was of a mother and father who not only lost their daughter, but four of her friends, all of whom were in the car with her when it crashed. That put a different perspective on my situation, made it look more mundane.

After about a year, I began to see that I was becoming more emotionally healthy, so I told the facilitator that I didn't need to come back; I was good. She agreed with me, but asked me to promise I would write this whole ordeal out, and then put it away. I did just that. I wrote and I cried, day after day, until I had it all down on paper. I have to say, when I finished, I was good.

I felt good knowing that if I ever needed to revisit that time in my life, I knew just where to go. It was all in one place instead of running around and around in my head, day after day. I was now free to move on in my life. I believe grief counseling is good, and can be even better when grounded in your faith.

———

Inspiration

Often in my writing, I've said that this really isn't about me. I'm not writing to be the center of attention or to attract sympathy. Yes, it is a story about me, but it could very easily be about many, many others. However, I can only know myself; I can't be sure how others think, or write, or how inspiration, so to speak, comes to them. For me, I believe the Holy Spirit is speaking through me. In many, if not all, instances, as I write, I am simply putting the words on paper. I can actually feel the spirit at work in me, and the words flow. They aren't even really my words, but the spirit at work through me. Later, when I read the words back, I am often astounded at the message – many times, a double message. One if you are a believer; another if you are not. Remember: eyes that do not see and ears that do not hear. When I am moved by this spirit, it all happens very quickly, and before I realize what is happening, it is done. I hope you recognize the passages as I now do.

———

Further Thoughts: Alone

Earlier in this narrative I wrote about my sense of being alone. I thought I had finished with that idea, but it appears that it hasn't finished with me. I'd like to add some thoughts now, to extend and develop that theme.

First:

There are times when you are completely alone, when no one but you and your doctor are present. To be awake during certain procedures is scary: just your voice and that of the doctor, who has more authority, more control, than you do. Those times couldn't pass quickly enough for me, and I think I've been lucky not to have encountered too many know-it-all medical professionals. You can have the most devoted, supportive, and caring husband imaginable, and still be alone as they do the biopsies, or as you enter that long tube, for 30 minutes at a time, one scan at a time. I think: "I've only got me right now. It's up to me. Again."

Second:

The one thing I have heard from everyone, and something that I myself have voiced many times over the past eight-and-a-half years, is the desire to have someone who understands the depths and the pain. Yet no one can. There is such a yearning for this that can surface in your mind at any time, in any place. I have told my husband this, time and again. I remember my hairdresser telling me after her husband passed away from cancer: "All he ever wanted was for me to feel what he felt, to truly understand. I told him I couldn't do that." Until you personally experience your own dying, you apparently cannot know.

———

Further Thoughts: My Mind

Is my mind going to give out on me? I've made some peace with my deteriorating body, but I now find my mind unable to do simple things. Physical pain robs me of my thinking self, in much the same way as the morphine, in higher doses, robs me of coherent thought. I am the one who has been "on top of my game" with medications, listening to what the doctors and nurses say, which is sometimes very different from what family members hear. I need to feel more secure in knowing someone has my back when I am unable any longer to be in charge of my medications.

A Paradox:

I can only keep on going when I know the end, the number of days I must continue on like this. Yet no one can answer this for me. I recognize a familiar tension between a strong desire to put on a good face, and the need to give myself a break while in the grip of critical illness and pain.

I can't go on.

I go on.

———

May 25 2018

Yes, May 25th of this glorious new year! I can hardly believe it. I am doing all I can do to stay here longer. Oxygen and sleep: my two favorite things. And this: a surprise visit from my sister-in-law, my new sister, Jill!

What an occasion it was. I just wanted to hold on to her and make sure she was real. I do close my eyes sometimes and I'll see someone, or something, so clearly, but when I open them, my vision hasn't been confirmed in reality; it was all in my head. I assume morphine and other drugs provide these visions, these imaginings, but in this case, I really didn't want to lose her. My brother-in-law Michael was standing there also, which made Jill seem a little more real. But, I thought, she's supposed to be at home in Colorado, not standing here in my Pennsylvania kitchen.

I am truly blessed to have a family like this. A sister-in-law who would travel so far just to put my book in my hands. She had chosen a stopping place, and with the help of her daughter-in-law, Alison, had the manuscript formatted and printed, with a beautiful cover design bearing my title and my name: Chasing After the Wind, by Susan "Micki" Digby. Jill's husband Marshall was also complicit in the surprise; he insisted that the only way to present the book was in person, so he bought her a plane ticket and sent her to me.

This is just the latest gift of kindness I've been given throughout this long journey. I've never been really comfortable receiving; even now, I'm still trying to figure out what I can do for others. Maybe I've been selfish my whole life and I don't know how to do it. I have mentioned this before; we all need to understand why we are here. I believe one purpose, one reason for being, is to enhance the lives of others, and of course, if given the opportunity, to introduce others to Christ. So, Jill, I am calling you out, sister. I wish to be more like you.

—————

June 1st

Another month has passed. Amazing. I watch the calendar, the hours of each day, wondering when I can be rid of this pain and suffering. Yes, suffering. My mornings are a reminder of my inability to do simple things. I am scared. As the day progresses, after I sleep at least two hours in the afternoon, my pain subsides and I can walk upright. I use what energy I have to help with dinner, eat dinner, and then take a shower. I try to have things to do that make me think, so I can stay awake. I haven't been very successful at that lately, as I tend to nod off frequently until bedtime arrives, around 10 PM. Working on the computer, I go right to sleep, and push all the wrong buttons! I am reading two great books, but they quickly put me to sleep as well. I see all of these as signs that I am failing, getting to the end of my time on earth. I am okay, just scared. When you can't breathe, you tend to panic. I have many of these episodes of momentary panic during the day. Even the short walk from the dining room to the bathroom requires time to recover, because It's so hard to breathe.

The tumor in my chest is undoubtedly the major cause of my increasing discomfort, and the acceleration of symptoms. This growing mass is causing fluid retention in my chest, neck, and face. And now there are two rope-like things on either side of my neck.

My oncologist's PA says they indicate a blockage, so my body has created two new blood vessels. God's creation, the human body, can even fix itself. I have witnessed that, and marveled.

I really do not want to be afraid of this process. I know God is in control. I tell myself: give it up to him. I love what God can do much more than what I can dream up. We all rest in his mighty hands, and he will use our gifts according to his purposes. Many times, we don't even recognize our own gifts, so why hold on to a control we only imagine? Give it up. Relax. This is what I must remember always.

———

June 2, 2018

My daughter Denise is coming to stay for a night. It is always good to see her and get some her energy. Boy, does she have energy! Our grandson Matthew is coming over on Tuesday, and we'll celebrate his 16th birthday with lunch, a cake, and gifts. He is so special. A gifted athlete, he wants to be a professional baseball player. He has two years of high school remaining, and I have no doubt he will achieve his dreams. On Thursday, my granddaughter Amanda is coming for dinner. We mentioned a special recipe of ours for sausage and she was quick to say she wanted to come. What almost-19-year-old wants to hang out with her grandparents? That alone makes Amanda dear to our hearts.

———

Thinking Back to the Very Beginning

To set the scene: it is a week before Christmas. My brother and his family are spending the holidays with us, and I find out, almost inadvertently, about this mass in my right lung. My primary care physician gives me the name of a thoracic surgeon, so I begin calling this man, Dr. Kucharczuk, trying to get an appointment to see him as soon as possible. I call repeatedly, leaving message after message, but no one calls me back. I continue to call, day after day, while traveling with my brother's family to New York and Connecticut, finally landing back at home for Christmas. We see an advertisement on television for Cancer Treatment Centers of America, and decide to call them. Because the size of the mass is so big, they agree to see me right away. My appointment is immediately after Christmas, and of course I go, and Richard goes with me. Initially, we are told by the head of oncology at CTCA that nothing can be done for me. We are in shock, double shock. But they then suggest that we spend three days there for scans, a biopsy, and other tests. So we do this, wandering around like zombies, doing what we are told, seeing each of the people who are to interact with us.

The very last of these people is a pastor, a Presbyterian pastor. As soon as we walk into his office, he begins our transformation. He tells us straightaway that we don't have time for a pity party; it's time to get over feeling sorry for ourselves. We have to be strong now. We have to fight. This caring man is so clear and strong in his message; he stresses that I am not a statistic, Nor is my outcome yet ordained. Wow! Did we get a wake-up call. Pastor Michael Barry also let me know how fortunate I was, because I could reach people through cancer that even he, as a pastor, could not. I had a new mission. We walked out of his office with our heads held high.

We knew we had one more appointment to get all the results of the scans, blood work, and other tests, and we were dreading it – expecting the worst. The CTCA oncologist, even before all the tests, had told us there was nothing he could do for me. But at this appointment the story had changed. We were told that surgery was an option, and I was being referred to the University of Pennsylvania – to a Dr. Kucharczuk. We told them we had been trying, without success, to get an appointment with this doctor for weeks. Just like that the door was open. They called and set up an appointment for the very next day. Amazing. We had hope again.

June 13, 2018

Getting up in the morning is sometimes the hardest thing I do all day. I always have plans for my day, yet dread what used to be the simplest tasks – getting cleaned up and dressed – which are no longer simple at all. Today, I plan to write. I need to write. Things have changed in my body. So much more pain, but now it is in my chest, where they discovered a new tumor growing about eight months ago. Moving at all causes great pain, so writing sounds pretty good: only my hand and arm need to move. Having something to do each day, even if it is in my mind, has helped me survive.

Having family around me is exhausting but wonderful. I am so blessed to have them wanting to do things, to help us, and to just sit and talk about their lives. My older daughter, Denise, has been staying at her sister Jenifer's house for several days, and has found things to do at our house each of those days. So we really have had some good time together. How I would describe this time: laughter and tears.

Since I am unable to go anywhere, each of our birthday people have come to us so we can celebrate them. We baked a cake for a lunch with our eldest grandson. He's 16! He got his driver's permit on his birthday, too. What a wonderful young man Matthew is. He is so good-looking, the girls are after him, plus he is very smart. He's great inside and out.

Yesterday morning, as we were having breakfast, the doorbell rang. A surprise visit from one of my former bosses and his wife, who now live in North Carolina. We always enjoyed their company when they lived here, but haven't seen them in some time. In they came, with lovely flowers for me. Richard was still in his pajamas – what a hoot! As luck would have it, I at least was dressed, although I hadn't brushed my teeth or combed my hair. They ended up staying almost two hours, and I was exhausted when they left. Like many people who see me, they said, "Well, you look good, so it's nice to know how well you are doing." Well? Me? I do not feel at all well. But I forget: you cannot see my pain. (Therefore it is not there to others.) Please don't get me wrong; I appreciate these folks.

Their sentiments are in the right place. They do care about me or they wouldn't go out of their way to come, bringing flowers and spending their time. This happens a lot.

Our younger daughter, Jenifer, and Amanda, our eldest granddaughter, came for dinner yesterday also. Jenifer told us that when she rides her bike, she often uses that time to pray and to talk with God. She is having a tough time with my illness, my suffering, and ultimately with my dying. She has been dealing with this for months now. So, in her conversation with God the other day, on her bike, she said, "But she's my mother," and God said, back to her, "She's my daughter." Jenifer has never had an experience like this. We were all touched, and became very quiet. Another reason why I am so blessed.

In retrospect, my visit with the hospice nurse on Monday was humorous. When he came this week, before we did anything, I said, "Is there any way of speeding this process up? My dying, I mean."

Well, he went into overdrive, coming up with all sorts of alternatives to "speeding it up." He suggested I get out more, several times. He wanted to schedule a social worker to come; he wanted to schedule a pastor visit. I told him I couldn't, I wouldn't, commit suicide, that I didn't believe in it. But he had already gone down that rabbit hole. He packed up his stuff and I had to remind him he hadn't even taken my vitals yet. So he did that and then suggested he come back Friday. I said "no" to everything so he left, but I think I am now more worried about my nurse than he is about me. Funny.

———

June 15, 2018

I know I am getting worse, week by week. It is noticeable not only to me, but apparently to others as well. Sleep is my refuge, far more than medication, although they have doubled my Tylenol for pain. Today, when my hairdresser hugged me, I felt it was the last time I would see her. She is so wonderful – comes to the house for me, and has for years. I hear of a trip my brother is planning to see me at the end of June, and his whole family can come at the end of July. My pastor commented that it was all about me now.

Am I too sensitive to others and picking out words that fit my narrative? There is no playbook on how to die. I really don't know what I am supposed to be thinking or doing.

———

June 17

I am thinking of all the things that need attention before I die. I have been doing this for a long time now, but this time I feel death is imminent. I am centering in on mid- to late-July. I have listened and heard about everyone's vacation schedule, and have asked my brother to come then with his family. We have made our lists of people to call when I die. I have some notes on my memorial service. I have written some notes to family members. Decisions need to be made regarding location and food. I feel as though my husband and caregiver may feel overwhelmed by all my family members, all high-achieving, Type A personalities. Of course, these are my plans, and God has a sense of humor, as we all know. I guess I just need to feel as though I am a part of it happening.

> *We don't receive wisdom,*
> *we must discover it for ourselves*
> *after a journey that no one can take for us –*
> *or spare us.*
> – Marcel Proust

———

June 25

One more day and my husband Richard's birthday. I am getting them all in, one way or another. Denise's birthday started well in advance with a 50s celebration in Florida with other 50-year-olds. Jenifer attended that big party, but is unable to attend the one

Spencer has planned closer to the actual date, with 50 guests. So Jenifer put together a gathering of family to celebrate (another surprise) on Saturday evening. After cocktails at our house, they went out for dinner. Sunday, they were back for lunch and my pastor joined us.

We will see what tomorrow brings for his birthday. I know Jenifer will be here. Amanda's birthday is two days later; my brother-in-law, Marshall's, is July 14, and done!

So now, I am looking for the dates of vacations. I believe after the second week of July all are home and accounted for. It might be the perfect time for a memorial service. I don't mean to be planning it, but I am.

———

July 3 2018

Oh, and my brother and his family are visiting the east coast for two weeks in July. I am most grateful that they understand where I am in this journey. I simply cannot entertain in any way. Things have gotten worse since I last wrote anything. First, I thought I had wax build-up in my left ear. I had it flushed, but the hearing loss continued to progress. Now I'm waiting for my nurse to acquire some device she needs to better assess the problem. That should happen the day after tomorrow. It has already been well over a month. Could be nerve damage, or another tumor. So then I was reading about the side effects of one of the drugs I am taking to remove excess fluid: hearing loss. Is that it? Another puzzle, just trying to keep up with physical symptoms, causes and effects.

And of course, God is talking to. me. I believe it – can you? Consider this:

Jenifer, my younger daughter, was visiting the other day and she said two things that needed to be said. They just slipped into our conversation.

She asked me, "Are you ready, Mom?"

I answered her, "Yes."

Then maybe a minute later she told me that she would be all

right; everyone would be okay; I could go; no worries.

Then she was gone. Only later did it fully dawn on me what she had said – what it meant – and it was such a relief to me. Again, someone who understands what I need. Later, I sent her an email thanking her. She didn't remember saying those things. Here I thought she had said them on purpose. Who was speaking to me? I believe it was God. As my daughter was saying, we seem to have an open dialogue with God right now.

———

July 5

I saw the nurse practitioner today. She found no wax in my ear, no visible obstruction, and didn't think it was the drug I'm taking, so – another tumor? Perhaps a fluid build-up similar to the one in my chest, face, and neck. These are the side effects that are not written down anywhere. So I have hearing loss. Another loss? We are working on ways to communicate. Touch is good. Other than that, my world is one of increasing silence.

———

July 6

Fifty years ago today, I gave birth to my first child. Everything about Denise speaks to being different, creative, strong, and good – everything to be proud of. She has become such a beautiful creation of God. I am so grateful that he chose me to mother her. She is truly beautiful, inside and out. In turn, God has chosen her to mother a couple of beautiful young women who are in need of her gifts for sure. The circle of life.

This is hard to write – both physically and emotionally. I will die soon. I know it. I struggle just to walk across the room. It is very hard to breathe. Now that is scary. I believe I have done everything or at least identified those things that need to be done. Life goes on. People figure out these things. After all, I did. Now, I write a few words, and then I sleep for 20-30 minutes. I am grateful to God for my wonderful life, my amazing family.

———

Micki died on October 30, 2018. Her husband Richard, daughters Denise and Jenifer, and granddaughter Amanda were all by her side. Her last words were, "I love you. I love you. I love you."

Appendix: Notes and Letters to Loved Ones

After her death, Micki's family discovered one further notebook, a collection of notes and letters that she had been composing in parallel with the narrative she sent to me. In fact, the first entry is about just that:

> Part of my plan is to journal often, and I have a purpose in mind – a selfish one at that. I am in search mode – looking for inspiration to show me a new thing, a way, a purpose. I had shed the old one in 2008 (pre-cancer) to make way for the new. At the heart of it sits a distant fear that I will become even more of a recluse – an island unto myself.
>
> For remembrance, I record here a couple of useful lines from Randy Pausch's "Last Lecture":
>> *The reason for the brick wall is to see how badly you want something.*
>> *Experience is what you get when you didn't get what you wanted.*
>> *Failure is not just acceptable. It is essential.*
>
> So, I am open to and searching for some inspiration which will lead me in the direction I am meant to pursue. There is no doubt in my mind that I can do "whatever it is," no matter how hard it is. I have always learned how to do and usually master, the skills needed to do whatever I did. It is now just a question of "what"? Sometimes through the act of writing one finds inspiration and thoughtfulness. Thus, I am pursuing this project as one avenue that Is open to me.

———

Following this statement of intention, Micki used the notebook to record letters to those she loved, along with some additional thoughts and quotations. It seems to me, these last letters are another form of the "Last Lecture" or the "ethical will" or the personal memoir – call it what you will. Not everyone is given to lengthy personal reflection (or a gifted editor!) but most of us are capable of writing at least a few short lines to those who will carry on after we are gone. These final meditations and benedictions – expressions of love, regret, and hope – comprise one more precious gift from Micki to those she loved, and who loved her.

Here are some excerpts:

To her elder daughter:

Some words for Denise
    Wow! You are one strong lady! All that you have been through – trying to have a baby (endless disappointments) – chronic illness (daily living with Lyme disease) – and you are living – not just alive. I know the difference, like you. Marta is a blessing in disguise, but you may not know this for a few more years. She tries your soul, for sure.
    I love you deeply. We are different in so many ways, but alike, also, in others. I am proud of the woman you have become. Continue to always be you. You are unique in so many ways.
    I want to say I am sorry for all the times I have caused you worry. I am strong – like you – and keep on keeping on even when it seems to be all uphill. I feel your love, and know you would do anything for me. It means peace to me, which is so precious these days, when there is so little of it in my life.
    I wish you love, always, and Spencer to care for you. He is special to bear the burdens he has carried also.
    I want you all to know that I wish I could jump in my car and come see you. To do for your families the things I dreamed I would do – am now unable to do – it hurts me. I only hope it doesn't hurt you. Please forgive me if you can. I failed all of you in this time of my life.
    I love you,
    Mom

To her younger daughter:

Note to Jenifer

I am so proud of you and who you have become! I'm not even sure how to write what I think, when I think of you. You are a beautiful, caring person – a woman! Wow, how did that happen? I remember you still as a little girl . . . But you are a mother, now, with a little girl of your own, who is growing up, and two little boys, who are "becoming" also.

I am sorry for the last couple of years – the worry I have caused you. Not a day goes by that you don't call and ask, "How are you?" I know from this how deeply my illness has caused you to worry. I wish it wasn't so. But at the same time, I know you because you are like me in this regard. You need to know, and to know the truth – the cold, hard facts – so you can be at peace. I am only sorry to have caused you so much worry and pain, but I am honest with you because I know you "have to know." Actually, I love this about you. I just wish I could always have good news.

Also, please know that it causes me so much pain to not be able to do all I want to do – for you, for your family. I have failed you all in that area. I do try to do all I can, but sometimes I feel overwhelmed by disease, treatment, pain – too tired, sometimes, to move. Please forgive me. I love you, Jenifer.

Mom

On another page, this quotation:

> We don't receive wisdom.
> We must discover it for ourselves
> after a a journey that no one can take for us or spare us.
> – Marcel Proust

Dated 8/2/2014, a cry, seemingly to herself:

I have become a prisoner of my own stronghold, of my

loneliness, confined therein. There seem to be wounds that time does not heal, maybe just reduces them to a manageable size. I am struggling to reclaim my world. "The new normal" seems to be getting smaller and smaller. Even in others' presence I feel lonelier and lonelier.

To her husband:

Richard:

You will never really know how bad I have felt, putting you through all of this knowing, and unknowing, and pain. Yes, I know – our pain – as I would have felt it if the tables were turned. Yes, we had many good times and many trying times, as everyone does. I remembered them well, even as you reminded me. We had a full life together – encountering everything! I have never felt that you planned well enough to give me complete peace, but then I don't expect you ever will – and now you won't even have my nudging you! You are a good man, strong but yet weak – which is good. You must know both to be a man. I have always loved you, sometimes more than others, as I am sure is true of you also. You have been a great father (makes me proud) and your grandchildren love you for who you are. And even dogs love you (which always made me wonder about me). So, you will do well on your own. I have tried to prepare you as best I could. I have so little energy – and in that I am sorry – for I have failed you, too! I feel bad about that. So little energy to start anything new; so little energy to do simple things. I always hope the next day will be better, but so far that hasn't happened. So, remain yourself and you will be happy – that is your nature. Your daughters will take care of you – each in their own way. Let them.

I love you,
Micki

There were loving, encouraging notes to her grandchildren: Marta, adopted by Denise and Spencer; and Amanda, Matthew, and Nicholas, the children of Jenifer and Michael. There were open-hearted – at times even light-hearted – notes to her two cherished sons-in-law. To Spencer: "When New York showed up at your wedding, in sunglasses, I should have known that this would be a different journey." To Michael: "I haven't always been the mother-in-law that I envisioned I would be, but I want you to know I tried my hardest to be my best. It just wasn't always good enough for me. I think you'll get that." To her brother Joe and and his wife, LuAnn, she speaks of abundant love, tempered with regret that they had not remained closer over the years. To their daughter, Sarah, there is unalloyed pride in her accomplishments, and hope for a bright future. In a note to Richard's brother, Michael, she calls him another brother to her, and describes their shared experiences and their shared worries over children and grandchildren. She ends by asking him to "keep an eye out for your brother. We both love you dearly."

To me, she wrote this:

Dear Jill,

Who would have known? We were rocking along as sisters-in-law for too many years, wouldn't you say? Now that we are "sisters" it feels so much better.

I do believe that we (you and I) had nothing to do with our coming together to do the book. God is all over it!

You and Marshall have raised three beautiful children – they will always be children to me. No matter where they go or what they do, they cannot fall out of favor with me.

So, does it feel like we've known each other for more than 50 years? So much of that time went by while we were traveling the world, pursuing our careers, and raising our families. I am truly blessed to have been given this opportunity to know you more. What if I had said "No"? What if you had said "No"?

Life is good for both of us. I am grateful and I love you, Jill,
Micki

Afterword

Several months before her death, I was still trying to push back against Micki's conviction that cancer is a solo journey. I'd received a new packet and had been weighing whether to include the latest passage on that theme. Gently, but with a bit of exasperation, I sent her the following email:

I had one more thought about "Alone." There's always at least one other presence with you, wherever you are, whatever you're going through. Call on Him. He'll always be beside you.

She replied:

Reminders are always good, thank you! I can get caught up in the present pain, I'm afraid.

This exchange brought to mind a hymn that I had sung, and recorded, with the William Ferris Chorale many years ago, when I lived in Chicago. In his haunting, inimitable style, Bill had composed an exquisite chant on the text of the 91st Psalm. Marshall dug out the old CD and managed to transfer the appropriate cut to my computer, and I sent it along to Micki. I encouraged her to use the refrain, "Be with me Lord, when I am in trouble," as a calming mantra in times of pain, anxiety, or uncertainty. She loved the hymn, and the message, and promised to take it to heart.

Be With Me, Lord, When I Am In Trouble

You who dwell in the shelter of the Most High,
Who abide in the shadow of the Almighty,
Say to the Lord: "My refuge and my fortress,
My God in whom I trust.

Be with me, Lord, when I am in trouble.

No evil shall befall you, nor shall affliction
Come near your tent,
For to his angels he has given command about you,
That they guard you in all your ways.

Be with me, Lord, when I am in trouble.

Upon their hands they shall bear you up,
Lest you dash your foot against a stone.
You shall tread upon the asp and the viper;
You shall trample down the lion and dragon.

Be with me, Lord, when I am in trouble.

Because he clings to me, I will deliver him;
I will set him on high because
He acknowledges my name.
He shall call upon me, and I will answer him;
I will be with him in distress;
I will deliver him and glorify him.

Be with me, Lord, when I am in trouble.

This wasn't the only song that inspired and consoled Micki toward the end of her life. Off and on, through the last months, we had an oblique email conversation about music for her memorial service, which she was planning. She sent me the lyrics to "Blessings" and asked if I would be comfortable singing it. She didn't say, "at my funeral," but I knew that's what she had in mind. In fact, "Blessings" wasn't quite my style, or in my soprano range, so I countered with "You'll Never Walk Alone," from Rogers and Hammerstein's *Carousel*. She immediately acknowledged the aptness of the lyrics, and I knew then that I'd have one last chance to tell Micki that with faith, hope, and love, no one ever walks alone.

Micki stopped writing about three months before her death. It had become too difficult to sustain the effort. There was too much pain to sit upright, even for short periods, and if she medicated the pain away, she couldn't stay awake. Her mind remained clear, but gradually she retreated within it, unable to hear; speaking very little. I like to think she was gathering herself for the journey to come.

On October 30, 2018, after almost nine years in the fight, Micki slipped gently from life to death. The end was peaceful; her family gathered near. At that moment, perhaps the Lord greeted her with these words: "Be with me, child. Your trouble is ended."

Jenifer Jill Digby Gile
At Liberty
Denver, Colorado
October 2018

Some Final Words
From Richard

In the more than 52 years that Micki and I were together, almost 51 of them in marriage, I always had the feeling that she had a sixth sense, a connection to a power greater than this world. As we started the last nine years of our journey together, we received the shocking news that Micki had lung cancer. We plunged into a world unknown, frightening, and chaotic, much like a roller-coaster, careening out of control. Emotions ran the gamut: from tears of self pity to hopes of a cure; from doubting decisions made to fearing opportunities lost. We heard these terrifying words: "There is nothing we can do for you." And these: "I think I can help you." We reeled from the results of one scan to the next, sometimes with deepening anxiety, sometimes elated by the slightest improvement. Hope and each other, that's all we had to hang onto.

The next four years, while anything but routine, did have a pattern: nine months of waiting for the scan that inevitably showed some change, then three months of treatment. As we approached our fifth year, I can still hear Micki's voice telling me, "You need to help yourself to help me." I thought I'd been handling things just fine (male ego) but now I listened. One Wednesday morning, I entered a room of other caregivers, a room no one wants to be in. Two hours later, I left both humbled and honored that I had been chosen to care for my wife, God's gift to me. Now it became my privilege to do God's work here on earth.

Micki was right that I needed help helping her, but how did she know? That sixth sense? She would often say, "It's such a nice day today. You should ride your bike." Or later: "You need to get out. You like people – why not try driving for Uber?" Or: "You are so good with people, how about serving the church as deacon?" To all of these suggestions and many more I answered, "Yes." I came to realize once again that although she had always been a master at understatement, she was able to get the job done by nudging me ever so gently in the right direction. This is one of the things I miss so much.

After her second course of chemotherapy, Micki had great difficulty even walking by an infusion room, even if she wasn't scheduled for treatment. A therapist friend met with us together, then with Micki alone, trying to determine the root cause of such psychological anguish. Using the technique known as EMDR (Eye Movement Desensitization & Reprocessing) Micki was able to identify the original trauma, which stemmed, not from her own treatment, but from her mother's death more than 20 years earlier. At that time, she'd been advised to "write it all down" and then put those writings aside. That process had been cathartic, and Micki had been able to move on. With this new anxiety reaction, the act of writing again allowed Micki to continue infusions. At this point, she was able to move into Immune Therapy, which originally had been denied her because of the lack of appropriate markers. The new treatment gave us almost two years of NED, (No Evidence of Disease).

Early in the journey, a good friend had penned these words in a note to Micki: "It is when you are at the deepest chasm in life that you are closest to the One who holds you in the palm of His hand." Approaching our last year together, Micki was carefully, systematically preparing us all for her departure from this life. There were many gentle nudges and a few clear requests, but all were delivered with her characteristic understatement. It was then that I realized something profound: as Micki's world steadily grew smaller – the less she could do physically – those very limitations were enlarging her spiritual life and bringing her closer to God. He was holding her, and she was resting ever so gently in the palm of His hand. Her faith was rock solid, an answer to prayer. It is that faith which now provides me with the strength and courage to carry on. As the many wonderful memories increase in my consciousness, I hear very clearly her last words to us all: "I love you. I love you. I love you."

Forever yours,
Richard

Joey and Sue circa 1950

pageant photo

wedding day: December 16, 1967

family photo

with my brother-in-law and sister-in-law, Marshall and Jenifer Gile, 2003

with my brother and his wife, LuAnn

my daughters, Jenifer and Denise

Richard's 70th birthday celebration

with my grandkids, Matthew, Nicholas, Marta, and Amanda

with Richard, Michael, and my grandkids

enjoying a quiet moment at Andrew Carnegie's Skibo Castle

Made in the USA
Lexington, KY
08 July 2019